To Jess
with n,
wishes - Ollie x

CW00487118

About the author

Oliver Cross was born in 1950 and brought up in
Lincolnshire, although he's spent most of his life
in Leeds. He graduated in politics from Leicester
University and has worked as a reporter and
sub-editor for the Gainsborough News,
Western Daily Press, Yorkshire Post and
Yorkshire Evening Post.
His hobbies include gawping and stapling.

Cats & Other Party Animals

By Oliver Cross

Published by York Place Media
York Place Media, Lion House, 41, York Place,
Leeds LS1 2ED West Yorkshire England

First published 2013

Book design: York Place Media

Printed in England by Jellyfish Solutions Ltd.
Swanmore, Hants.

ISBN: 978-1-909826-02-1

Contents

To Lynne, who knows what I'm like.

INTRODUCTION

My friend Ron, who doesn't know the meaning of tact, once told me I was a paradox.

He said there were plenty of people, particularly journalists, who could talk very well but couldn't write an interesting sentence to save their lives.

I on the other hand, although enormously dull to talk to, could occasionally create an interesting written sentence.

Encouraged by this, I've looked back over my many years of writing a weekly column for the Yorkshire Evening Post to find some sentences of which Ron might approve.

It's only a small and random part of my output because I don't keep proper files but I have tried to put each article into some sort of context, remembering that things change faster than you think.

Looking back, I became aware that there's a divide between the cheery-chappy of my earlier columns and the tortured soul that emerged following the banking crisis of 2008, after which I did little more than spend five years seething.

That should make things more interesting because unending cheeriness is a frightening prospect. You might, meanwhile, wish to console yourself with the thought that, according to Ron, whatever you think of my writings, things would be so much worse if you were to listen to my talkings.

ONE

Home discomforts

The house that caused so many problems was eventually sold at a huge profit during the unsustainable banking boom which ruined the rest of the country. Hooray for me.

A curse upon my house
About 12 years ago I bought a house in Bradford that has been a pain in the neck ever since, which is understandable because it's also been an albatross and a millstone round my neck and it would be unrealistic not to expect neck problems from it.

It was a quickie, unconsidered, panicky divorce-buy, which probably doomed it to unhappiness and failure from the start but at the time I thought it was a cheap and not, to be fair, unprepossessing, stone back-to-back house in a predominantly Asian area of Bradford.

I didn't realise, because the estate agents didn't think to tell me, that it had been cursed by all the gods of Bradford (which is quite a lot) unto eternity.

I didn't stay there long; I could just about stand it until wedding parties from the neighbouring Sikh temple started walking past and tormenting me by looking very happy, like people who had settled, organised family lives.

Circumstances changed and I left, transforming myself, so I fantasised, into a hard-as-nails, grasping absentee landlord.

At first I put the house into the hands of managing agents, which was a small shop in Bradford staffed entirely by people with no clue at all about property dealing. Once when, and not for the first time, the tenants did a bunk, I told the lady: "Well, at least we've still got the deposit."

She paused, as a decent acknowledgement that she was not really in the right job, before replying: "Er, I took the deposit as a payment of rent. He had a really nice face."

So I reckoned I could do her job better myself and immediately rented the house out to a gang of what I took to be Liverpool builders, although, being, as it proved, accomplished liars, they could equally have come from Surrey.

They paid the deposit in £20 notes, which is the finest sight in the world and one I had never seen before (this was about 1997), and when I paid my first rent-collection call, they had refurnished the place to a higher standard than I ever had achieved and suspiciously tastefully for Liverpool builders.

Then, when I went to collect the third rent-payment, I found they had stripped the house completely, including my furniture, their furniture and an enormous power-gym machine which the previous tenant, a dangerous psychopath, had erected in the attic before doing his bunk. It must have involved some clever dismantling and the thieves were very tidy, so I decided they were my best tenants so far.

Then I got a very nice single father with a distressed-looking daughter of about 14 or 15.

When the rent dried up I went to investigate and the owner of the local corner shop said he had last seen the girl being taking away in an ambulance. I waited for weeks before deciding that the house had reverted to its default position of unlet and rotting away, then cleared their possessions out.

This turned out to be harrowing; the girl had left a diary of her mental agony in the house which, although I couldn't bear to read much of it, was so sad that I couldn't bear to throw it away either. So I shoved it in the roof-space in case the nice father or the distressed daughter ever came back and realised that things weren't really that bad and learned to look back and laugh about it.

Which is not likely because the house is cursed and I don't think having an account of adolescent misery hidden inside it will improve its karma one bit.

For example, after a few other letting disasters (including the couple who did a bunk and, very appropriately I thought, stripped the house of absolutely everything except a print of Edvard Munch's The Scream) I thought I had got lucky.

The tenant was an elderly Hindu widower who worked in the mills of Bradford for about 50 years, became a foreman and brought up a son with a big-shot job and a BMW. That done, the old man decided to return to India and, while making the arrangements, foolishly stayed at my house for a few months.

He was a wonderful tenant; every time I went for the rent, he would explain how he had mended something I didn't know was broken and then, when he had handed over the money, he would ask me to come to the pub with him so he could buy me a pint.

The week he moved in, the two nearest pubs closed due to lack of custom ("It's all those flaming Muslims," he said bitterly). We found another, although it took him some time to hobble there, and we had some very pleasant rent-day outings .

The last time I saw him, though, he was thoroughly depressed. The house-curse was following him and in the week he was packing up for his move back to India, his homeland state ("just my bloody luck") brought in a law banning all alcohol, including even a nice pint of Tetley's. The nearest bar was now about 100 miles away.

However, I think things are about to change and, although I can't exorcise curses, I'm about to transform my house in Bradford from a disaster into an ideal starter home with convenient access to all local conveniences.

4

After the Indian widower left, I handed the house over to a charity association letting out houses to newly-released prisoners, which meant, although I had to give up all hopes of making any decent money, I also didn't have to personally speak to thieving tenants.

The charity association woman explained that the ex-criminals could be all sorts of people but she could guarantee there would be no habitual arsonists because who would want that sort of person in their house? (To which I wanted to reply "Me, especially if the arsonist was armed with a ton of TNT" but I let it lie.)

Instead she offered to let the house to everybody from rioters to paedophiles but I didn't want to know anything about my tenants – even when the housing association telephoned me to say they had had to call in specialist contractors to remove hazardous toxic waste dumped in the cellar which was endangering the whole street.

I didn't bother to ask for details. I've just waited for my regular rent cheque every month for the last couple of years, thinking that if any of the tenants were to catch the house curse, it would be no bad thing.

(One of my other great hopes was that, out of habit, one of the ex-convicts would stage a protest about his inhuman housing conditions and rip all the tiles from my roof, which would probably work to my advantage, insurance-wise.)

Now, however, the housing charity people have decided that they want to end the deal because they don't think it fair on criminals to leave them in such cursed conditions, and this week, because the estate agents seem to be selling places I wouldn't think of living in for prices I wouldn't dream of paying, I'm putting my house on the market.

My slogan will be: 'A happy home for happy people' because in my experience everybody involved in the housing market lies through their teeth at all times and on principle.

First drink your lager
On Sunday I made a water feature for my garden, this being the kind of thing, I thought, that a responsible suburban man should be doing over the weekend.

It's not the best water feature you'll ever see, but it cost nothing at all and took 40 minutes from conception to completion. Plus it's a reflection of my special character and ingenuity (or, as my sister said on seeing it, "bloody typical").

If you want to make one yourself, here's the recipe.

To begin the project, assemble the following: A water pump, a goldfish pond, your pebble collection, some green bottles (about 10 should do it), a few shells and the plaster-cast garden ornament of your choice. These will have to be placed in a special water feature bucket, which should have a 3cm diameter hole in the bottom and a U-shaped cut-out about 10 cm deep in its rim. Check to see whether you've got one in the garden – I did and

I found one I hadn't noticed before because it had been converted into a patio container containing a dandelion and some grass.

It's made of thick and heavy metal and originally came, I think, from a smelting factory. If you can't find one, simply convert one of your existing patio containers, remembering that you will be placing a hosepipe from the pump into the hole at the bottom so that water can percolate through your water feature accessories and then fall, in a calming feng shui manner, through the U-shape and back into the pond.

Now you can start the construction stage. First empty the container (the dandelion can be replanted in a well-drained, south-facing position and you should throw any woodlice from the container into the pond to see whether the goldfish will eat them, which they won't).

Next feed the hosepipe into your smelting vessel, sealing it with a product called No More Big Gaps. This you spray around the hole and it expands in a very watchable polystyrene-ish sort of way until it neatly embeds the pipe. Unfortunately it doesn't appear to be waterproof, so you could try Blu-Tack instead.

Then fill the vessel with green bottles. The bottles will give the feature an underlying limpid green aura which you will find very spiritual (if you have time, you could intensify the effect by removing the Sainsbury's French Lager labels). Next place your pebble collection over the bottles. I have seven pebbles, each with its own story to tell but since they don't quite cover the bottles, I have added to them my shell collection (three) and some yellow china ducks (optional).

Then top the whole structure off by selecting a garden ornament to sit in the middle of it. I have, though I'm not sure why, an enormous collection of garden ornaments but the choice came down to a Wise Chinaman or a Proud and Haughty Bird and I went for the Proud and Haughty Bird because I thought it looked more classy.

Unfortunately, I think it's also a fish eagle because, far from being spiritually uplifted by my water feature, the goldfish have gone back to the bottom of the pond and are looking very glum.

False washing syndrome

Just my blooming luck. I thought things were going fairly smoothly for the first time in 15 years then I went and caught Munchhausen's Syndrome.

Munchhausen's is actually rare in Britain because its sufferers, who have a morbid compulsion to seek medical attention, usually cure themselves pretty quickly when they see the queues at A&E.

In extreme cases they fake desperate diseases so they can have dramatic emergency operations, but they tend to cool off a bit when they realise it means joining a two-year waiting list. And it's no use going to a hard-pressed British GP and saying "I've got Munchhausen's syndrome and need unnecessary medical attention immediately" because he'll think you are just imagining it and tell you to go away.

8

Which is why many sufferers turn to the secondary form of the disease, called Munchhausen's syndrome by proxy, which is what I caught last week. This is when, having given up on getting any dramatic help for yourself, you pretend your children are desperately ill and then gratify yourself, by proxy, through all the attention the NHS will rightly give them.

I've had to drop the sick-children variation of the syndrome on the grounds that I always taught my own children that the only proper reason for going anywhere near a hospital is that you were taken there, comatose, in an ambulance.

And besides they've now grown up and have more sense than to collaborate with my morbid compulsions, so I've had to focus all my attention-seeking behaviour on to domestic appliances.

Which is why I felt compelled to call a washing machine repair man out for no reason at all last week, just so I could enjoy the thought of somebody worrying and working on my behalf.

Actually, he saw through me immediately and explained in a kindly way that the problem was essentially psychosomatic. What I had fooled myself into thinking was that the door wasn't closing properly and that my clothes were coming out looking hardly any cleaner than when they went in.

The first problem was due to the fact that I had, sub-consciously, adopted a hopelessly unviable door-closing technique and the second I blame on the advertising industry. They've built up my expectations so much that I expect to see a bright and billowing line of Persil washing in my back garden and can't accept the reality, which is more like Stalinist Poland.

I realise that eventually I will have to face up to my inner demons and confront my syndrome.

But it would have been kinder if the washing machine repair man, instead of acting like some sort of holistic therapist, had indulged me and made a fuss, banging his spanners around, shouting and swearing and doing nothing useful at all.

That's what you pay your call-out fee for.

Junk by numbers

Last week you didn't see me because I took a week off to hire a skip and clear out all my junk. (Tommy Cooper to builder's merchant: "Can you arrange a skip outside my house tomorrow morning?" Builder's merchant: "You can skip anywhere you like, sir. It's a free country.")

Anyway, I decided the best way of tackling things would be to arrange the junk into categories so that I could formulate a prioritised junk disposal policy with best-policy guidelines. This took until Friday afternoon but produced some interesting findings. Essentially junk consists of a) things which don't work anymore, b) things which never worked, c) embarrassing things, d) mysterious things and e) bits of wood.

The first two categories are mainly vacuum cleaners and kitchen implements, the third consists of, for example, mugs decorated with busty women who turn naked when you pour hot water into them (and I'm fed up of saying "I was being ironic petal, where's your sense of humour?")

The mysterious things are mainly bits of technology which have passed me by (including, for some reason, a Walkman which became totally redundant before I had worked out how to unwrap it). And the bits of wood are mainly things I rescued from skips thinking they would come in useful one day but which I have now returned to skip limbo.

TWO

You could make it up

The following piece is based on the 2002 Countryside Alliance insurgency against diesel prices and plans to out-law fox hunting.

Country pursuits

This week I've decided to raise the tone a bit

I'm compiling a Nature Diary because I saw a fox on the way to work in Woodhouse, Leeds, and now feel qualified to talk about rural affairs and join the Countryside Alliance. (It was me who was on the way to work, by the way, not the fox. Foxes don't go to work because they are idle vermin, as you would know if you were a country lover like myself).

Here starts the diary: As I meander over the plashy, waterlogged plains of Woodhouse Moor – how close to Leeds city centre and yet, with its trees and verdant meadowlands, how far – I espy my old enemy, Reynard the Fox.

Formerly the local people were wont to disport themselves at fairs and circuses on the Moor but the stout-hearted fairground folk have left, for the price of diesel and cruel cuts in EU subsidies

12

have driven them all to despair and no longer can we sample those simple delights of yore, such as hot-dogs cooked in sump oil.

The only presence on the moor this damp morning is Reynard, by far the most dedicated, ruthless and cruel adversary the honest folk of Woodhouse have ever encountered. The sly, red-pelted Bolshevik has moved in where once Woodhouse folk found their innocent pleasures in the buttercup bedecked grass, or sometimes behind trees.

I immediately send an e-mail to Tony Blair – but addressed, so I can be sure of him receiving it, to his best friend, Saddam Hussein – suggesting that, if he wants my vote, he should stop criticising simple inner-city country pursuits such as our four-month long annual fireworks festival, when we make loud bangs to scare the foxes away and stop them eating babies.

I try to correct his woeful ignorance of country affairs by suggesting that, instead of persecuting people forced to carry sawn-off shotguns and machetes for their own protection, he should concentrate on the real villain, ruthless Reynard himself.

There is no reply, of course. Perhaps I should have sent the e-mail to Blair's most valued ally, Adolf Hitler.

The next day is a crisp, glorious morning and I am walking past the back of Leeds University, just minutes from the city's shopping streets. To my left there is a charmingly indistinct sound which I at first mistake for a field vole disporting itself.

Foolish me! For soon I espy the truth. A pigeon, true to its charmingly vagabond nature, is vomiting on a half–eaten pizza.

To my right there is a fast-moving, intensely-directed brown blur which I at first mistake for a police marksman moving into position. Then I see those sharp, super-intelligent eyes and realise my error, for the chance of coming across a police officer with sharp eyes in this area is very low indeed.

It is, as I should have realised earlier, yet another fox. Bold as brass, threatening our very way of life and personally protected, it seems, by Mr Mussolini Blair himself.

I send an e-mail reminding Tony the Traitor that, although Woodhouse folk are slow to anger, our patience has its limits.

erhaps he won't find our plight so amusing when foxes start to infiltrate Debenham's and other leading department stores, as they surely will until we get a government which truly understands our ways.

The drone of a police helicopter momentarily eclipses the familiar harsh cries of the magpies collecting, as is their wont, their protection money.

The postman, still humming an ancient drum-and-bass melody from the night before, nears the front door and forces his blood-stained fingers through the jagged metal of the double-protection security grille and into the letterbox.

The letter is from the Prime Minister. Apparently Mr Blair cares very deeply about Britain's glorious countryside , although he doesn't think he can give me free diesel for life, as demanded.

I decide to give Mr Blair another chance and send him a memo pointing out that he could win the gratitude of the whole countryside by encouraging joy riders, drive-by assassins and other marginalised inner-city folk to target foxes rather than decent people like me.

THREE

My inner nerd

My alter ego Colin sometimes turns up in my columns when things are slow. Or in this case, rainy.

Colin the rainman

Colin, who represents a part of me I would rather ignore – the inner nerd with the emotional intelligence of an electric toothbrush – has surfaced again because, being a wholly misguided DIY enthusiast, he thinks he has some important topical tips to pass on. Over to you Colin…

Hi, Colin here. And the message as the wet weather sets in, is 'Don't be a drip!' or, to put it more practically, don't let the unusual rainfall levels create unnecessary psychological problems which might require medication.

The bad news is that many patio owners are at present feeling responsible for increasing the risk of flooding by leaving nowhere for their rainwater to run away.

Removing the patio is not always an option because many patio owners have already strained all their muscles laying the patio down, and to tear it up again would negate their health insurance. Al-

16

so some of them have patios which, if the under-surface were to be exposed, might attract intrusive questions from the police.

The solution is simple; leave the patio where it is and cover it with a 15cm layer of an absorbent, porous plastic, rubber or cellulose material, available in block form from Halfords or any reputable car-cleaning accessory supplier. To put it simply, it soaks up the rainwater in a way analogous to a sponge (would this be because it is a sponge? – OC).

And furthermore, disposing of the accumulated rainwater couldn't be simpler; simply wring out the absorbent blocks into your gutter or perhaps a convenient, flooded area when nobody's looking.

You will be transformed from an eco-failure to the reigning (or, if I may put it more hilariously, raining!) eco-champion.

Now to my next DIY wet-weather tip. This involves creating an umbrella-hat made from a conventional umbrella with the handle removed and replaced with the framework of a roughly head-sized lamp shade.

The umbrella-hat is immune from the presently prevalent blustery conditions because it is fixed by two large bolts which screw into each side of the temples and allow the wearer to do two-handed activities, such as knitting, while walking in the rain and looking very cool indeed.

And finally, here is my step-by-step... oh, I think I'm being strangled.

Liking it hot

This is the week when I normally produce my popular annual Christmas Gift Guide, alerting readers to a range of hot, hot buys to suit all budgets, tastes and personal profiles, although obviously within reason and excluding monks.

However, I've decided this year to hand the task over to my alter ego Colin, who, if you've met him in this column before, you will remember is very fond of DIY and banality, which makes him an ideal Christmas Gift Guide compiler.

Hi, Colin here – all 'present' and correct and ready with a range of exciting gift suggestions! Enjoy!

A gift for her: The ladies love nothing more than multi-tasking and will be instantly won over by the new Four-In-One ballpoint pen. Simply choose the colour you want – from a range including, well actually wholly composed of, black, blue, green or red – then use the simple colour-coded system to depress the relevant button and hey presto! a whole world of multi-tasking colour is at your fingertips and all in one pen. Comes with a fingernail-friendly operation system ideal for the modern lady.

A gift for him: We all know that men love gadgets and that, following the example of Jamie and Gordon, they also love messing about in the kitchen. So what better gift than a spoon rest? Supplied in a range of ceramic and plastic finishes, the spoon rest has been described in cool circles as the new butter-pat maker. Do not swallow.

A gift for teenagers: It's widely recognised that today's youngsters are so obsessed with studying to get A-stars and helping others that they often ignore the important things and leave school with no idea of, for example, how to refresh a tired door architrave or measure the water flow from a low-level cistern.

The answer is to buy the teenager in your family a piece of practical equipment which will inspire a life-long interest in DIY and my own suggestion would be one of those special rollers which allow you to paint the side of the radiator nobody can see. Practical, elegant and, to put in modern parlance, wicked, dude man.

FOUR

Points north

Since writing the following pieces, there's been news of huge finds of shale gas in the north of England. Extracting it may create serious environmental problems, but then it's only the north, innit?

Degrees of Kelvin

Whither Britain? Search me, although I really think it's time to ask the question, if only because if we leave things to drift, we could end up anywhere (metaphorically, I mean).

The question arises because the former Sun editor and bigmouth, Kelvin MacKenzie, sounding off in the Daily Telegraph, thinks that London and the home counties are being ripped off by layabouts from the rest of Britain, who slob around in their subsidised council houses watching Sky TV and stealing welfare payments from out of the mouths of stockbrokers (well, I'm paraphrasing, but not much).

He thinks there should be a new grouping, on the lines of Italy's Northern League, to look after the needs of "hard-working, clever and creative people living in London and the South-East."

We can dismiss MacKenzie's rantings because there could be no more toxic words on a CV than 'former Sun editor', but we still have to decide whether the Britain most of us grew up in is on its way out – and, in the case of Scotland, could be gone very soon.

The MacKenzie approach reflects a kind of South-Eastern triumphalism, a view (much encouraged, incidentally, by Tony Blair and New Labour) that the core of the country, the source of its wealth and moral probity, lies in a place called Middle England, which, apart from a few well-off suburbs, doesn't mean the English Midlands – they have been as much hit by industrial decline as the North – but rather, say, Buckinghamshire or Kent. Wales, Scotland and Northern Ireland exist only as problems.

I once visited the splendid non-conformist church built by Sir Titus Salt in his company village of Saltaire near Bradford. Sir Titus made his millions in a very northern way, by producing cloth for the world, including the South-East.

In the church, a woman volunteer helper who (this was a few years back) had worked in the mill when it still made textiles, said that one of Sir Titus's descendents, who was "very well-spoken and came from down south" had visited the church, although the visitor didn't look at all interested and left very quickly.

This shows how gravity works; money made in the north has been going south for centuries and it's what's built many a half-timbered Victorian mansion in Buckinghamshire. Southern talent and ability didn't come into it.

Mind you, if you were looking for Kelvin Mac-Kenzie's "hard-working, clever and creative" people, you wouldn't have to travel south; you'd be better looking at how hopeless northern dopes have created, in the industrial wasteland of Salt's Mill, one of the most stimulating buildings in the land.

But the lesson surely is that unless everybody takes a one-nation approach, the nation could fall apart. Southern right-wingers like MacKenzie might be in the ascendency at the moment, but (cross fingers) there could be a reckoning for the financiers and their hangers-on in London and the South-East.

The thing is that City types can collect all sorts of commissions and percentages from, say, the making of caravans, but someone still has to make caravans. The time may come when the old northern manufacturing model reasserts itself, in which case Kelvin MacKenzie would look as utterly irrelevant as he deserves to look.

(Afternote: this was written in December 2012).

Moving up in Lancashire

This week I've been travelling but only in a small way, because you don't need to go far to find whole new worlds – in this case Burnley, Lancashire.

Burnley has an enormous sense of its place, which is in a strip of cotton-manufacturing set-

22

tlements, also including Nelson and Colne, in east Lancashire; it's not a poor relation of Blackburn or Manchester and actually many Burnley people regard the Blackburn accent, which we think of as the definitive Lancashire accent, as being, as they would dismiss it, 'well funny'.

Anyway, this visit to Burnley, Lancs, was my first for years and years and was to a terraced street which, when I was last there, was quite distressed and might, through neglect, have tumbled down were it not for the fact that the stone mill cottages are very solid and so, as we shall see, are the stone mill cottage dwellers.

This street, home to my oldest (sorry, most longest-term) friend Kath, was the one where Paul Abbot, author of the TV show Shameless, was brought up.

All the goings-on on the Chatsworth Estate, including a regularly alcoholically-collapsed father and self-reared children, were rehearsed in this corner of Burnley.

When I first encountered the street it was a bit like that, although it was also pocketed by warm, decent, life-enhancing people, which sounds patronising but isn't because it was.

My return to Burnley demonstrated this. The street, Healey Wood Road, is on the very edge of town – cross it and walk a bit and you are in the middle of the Pennine hills. In between there is a scruffy area of old quarry land once occupied by abandoned caravans, cars, sheds, TVs and things you would rather not investigate.

23

Kath and two of her female neighbours bought a patch of land opposite their Healey Wood Road homes, cleared and enlarged it with creative planting and possibly creative land-grabbing and installed gravel paths, terraces and water features so now it's become a wonderland – more like the Chatsworth Estate, Derbyshire, than the Chatsworth Estate, Paul Abbot-land.

For example, Kath held an evening barbecue in the communal garden at the weekend and wondered which patio it should be held on so as to best catch the falling light.

Nobody in the history of Healey Wood Road has ever had to worry themselves about which patio to eat on; it's as unlikely a dilemma as wondering which paddock to exercise the ponies on.

Things have changed for the better, as, here and elsewhere over the last 10 years, things generally have, although you would have to extract toenails to get anybody to admit it. Windows are clean, woodwork painted, hanging baskets are looking jolly, and it was even rumoured, though not widely believed, that one of the nearby terraced houses had sold for £70,000.

(Afterword: This was written in September 2008. I suspect, in the north at least, that things might have slipped back since then.)

Unjust William

The Harrying of the North was William the Conqueror's successful campaign in the winter of

24

1069-70 to establish Norman rule from the Humber to the Tees.

The campaign was brutal and vindictive; whole villages were destroyed and agricultural land was salted to make it barren for decades.

By some estimates, more than 100,000 people were killed.

I was reminded of the Harrying (sometimes, and even more appropriately, called the Harrowing) of the North by last week's budget, although obviously, making allowances for scale, that was rather a hysterical reaction.

The Normans destroyed crops and livestock, leaving the northerners to starve or turn to cannibalism, while the budget merely imposed VAT on hot pies, pasties and sausage rolls – a move which disproportionately hit the north because the huge Greggs bakery chain, based in Newcastle, lost £30m off its share price as soon as the VAT changes were announced.

I can imagine the members of some treasury or cabinet committee looking horrified when told that a minor tax change could have such a big effect on one of Britain's most successful companies, while piling extra costs on the declining number of working people allowed out at lunchtimes.

But then an ex-Etonian intern pipes up, George Osborne-style, to point out that the VAT change will mainly hit low and middlingly-paid people in the north of England, where most Greggs shops are, and leave London-based financial services companies untouched, so where's the problem?

Which sounds like a vision fuelled by northern paranoia until you consider that another major budget change involved imposing VAT on static caravans rather than, say, yachts or helicopter pads.

It's as if the posh intern had again piped up with the astonishing information that 95 per cent of British static caravans are made in East Yorkshire, giving employment to around 6,000 people and that if you wanted, with one blow, to hit manufacturing, the north and a leisure industry mainly used by the sort of people who shop at Greggs, this would be the way to do it.

Another VAT imposition, on the rental for hairdressers' chairs, is free of north-south bias but again hits sometimes struggling working people trying to make a decent living and seems inspired by a mentality that dictates that "if you're going to pick a target, then pick a weak one.'

I don't suppose many hairdressers outside Knightsbridge have been to dinner with David Cameron.

All this is against the background of the government's new plan to fix public-sector salaries regionally, which will mean less pay in the poorer regions, which became the poorer regions because, just as in the 11th century Harrying of the North, governments in the 1980s followed a scorched-earth policy, leaving acres and acres of former steelworks, coal mines and shipyards derelict.

Successive governments since then have thought it only fair to try to correct the north-south disparity by directing public-sector jobs towards the north.

It's only now that they've concluded that the best solution is to deliver the north an extra kick.

Going underground

This week I discussed the differences between Leeds and Manchester while sitting in an ex-toilet in Manchester.

This, converted into a small but noisy bar, was one of those Victorian or Edwardian underground public toilets, surrounded by ornate iron railings, which once graced (although I don't think that's quite the word) the streets of our larger towns, until it was decided that the nation's bladder control had improved to such a remarkable extent that local authorities no longer needed to go to the expense of building handsome civic toilets, or indeed any toilets at all.

Anyway, the toilet conversation took place just opposite the grand, now rather dusty, Palace Hotel, into which you could fit most of Leeds's important Victorian buildings – barring the Town Hall, obviously – with ease.

Manchester, like Liverpool, is full of these great piles, a legacy of King Cotton, when there were fabulous fortunes to be made and, said Benjamin

Disraeli, Manchester was "the most wonderful city of modern times."

Leeds, meanwhile was keeping its nose to the grindstone and earning a good living through, among other things, flax processing, clothing, printing and, to the south of the city, world-class engineering.

It never got as rich as Manchester, nor as flashy, but when the old order collapsed and the great Victorian mills and factories started to vanish, Leeds – very dark and grim when I arrived here in the 1970s – fared better because of its diverse industrial base and very adaptable citizens.

Now flash forward, as I did on my rare visit to Manchester this week. The place was all dressed up for the current Manchester International Festival featuring, among others, Sinead O'Connor, Victoria Wood, Bjork and Damon Albarn, plus a full-scale production of Wagner's Die Walkure.

Manchester, it seems, particularly in view of the BBC's move to Salford, is trying to build a new base in what they call the creative industries – unnecessarily I think because all industries are, by definition, creative.

Meanwhile, Leeds keeps banging on about its remarkable prospects as a retail powerhouse, when high-street shopping has gone into a dive-bomb decline, or its prime position in the disgraced financial services sector.

It's not, despite all that childish Wars of the Roses Yorks-Lancs rivalry, a competition; but it may be time for Leeds to raise its game a little.

Stranded on the Mersey

I don't usually take much notice of cathedrals, although the Anglican cathedral in Liverpool is hard to miss, it being, by some counts, the fifth biggest cathedral in the world.

Which is a bit too big in practical terms, given that Anglican congregations had been in steep decline for decades before the cathedral, which had its foundation stone laid in 1904, opened in 1978, although I understand that practicalities aren't everything, because otherwise cathedrals would mainly be sited in low-rent industrial estates or former bingo halls.

Still, the Anglican cathedral did worry me, particularly because, for a relatively new building, it seemed already grubby, as well as being dull, bombastic and unenlightening.

It also looks rather stranded, like an ocean liner which has found itself in harbour after the tide's gone out .

The point about Liverpool, a city which people now think it's fine to make fun of, is that it was, as late as the foundation of the Anglican cathedral, one of the leading cities of the empire and the world.

This is why it can't help but have big ideas, even though it was revealed recently that Tory ministers in the 1980s thought the best solution to the problems of the city would be to abandon it to 'managed decline'.

Public buildings, especially pubs, are extravagant and theatrical in Liverpool; it's to do with once-

29

great wealth and maybe also with a Celtic (Irish and Welsh) heritage.

Now it seems that, not far from the magnificent waterfront, areas of dereliction are being put to rights, even though the latest waterfront building, the Museum of Liverpool Life, could, from the outside, have as easily been built in Skegness.

Mind you, and to be fair, you can't build the Liver Building twice.

A death in the city

At the weekend I came across a grim sight – the half-demolished remains of Tetley's brewery in Leeds.

The curious thing about the brewery, which I haven't seen for months, is that it looks bigger, and in a way more impressive, as a half-demolished shell than it ever did as a working site.

There are enormous piles of bulldozed masonry and ripped-up metal – I couldn't believe the old place could have contained so much shiny metal, once, I suppose, channelled through vessels and pipes to produce a river of beer and lager which made lots of people, particularly in Leeds, very happy... until some spoil-sport explained that beer should only be enjoyed in homeopathic quantities.

There's a lesson here about the transience of things which seem solid and indestructible – as Rudyard Kipling put it, although he forgot to mention breweries:

Cities and Thrones and Powers
Stand in Time's eye,
Almost as long as flowers,
Which daily die...

I think that when I moved to Leeds in the 1970s, the idea that Tetley's brewery could be reduced to a scrapyard – except as a prelude to building an even grander brewery in some other part of Leeds – would have seemed ludicrous.

Which is why I found it somewhat shocking to see it smashed up and waiting to be melted down and recycled into something a lot less socially useful than a good brewery.

All this, of course, is ultimately to do with the slow death of industrial Britain, where large factories supported large breweries and pre-globalised cities, not feeling a need for virgin olive oil or Chilean wine, were happy to survive on local products like beef dripping and Tetley's.

The half-flattened brewery is not so much a sad sight for beer drinkers (and actually I never much liked Tetley's ales) as a sad sight for Leeds – it's as if the Town Hall had been converted into flats or the Parish Church into a carpet warehouse.

FIVE

Product placements

These pieces were written in the early 2000s, when shopping was a bigger thing than it was before we ran out of money. I don't think the philosophy of marketing has changed much, though.

Viva Vivality
What would help to make the world a better place would be a lot more Vivality, an exciting new range of hair care products brought to you by Wella.

Actually, it's the word I'm interested in rather than the shampoo, which is sold under the slogan 'If you've got it, you'll know it', which I think you probably would, since it doesn't come cheap enough to buy by accident.

Probably other people would know it too, because, according to the Wella girl used in the advertisement, it makes you look immensely smug and causes you to walk around with your head permanently bowed so as to show off the Vivalityness of the top of your hair.

But don't expect me to buy it, because I've never quite seen the point of hair-care products, relying, at the moment, on Safeway's family bath soap, which I think smells quite nice at the price.

It's true no woman has ever thrown herself at me on account of my Vivalitynaciousness, but neither have I been expelled from any fashionable social group or posh city bar entirely because of my dull, lifeless hair.

But back to the word, which I presume is supposed to suggest both vitality and vivaciousness in a way which could only have been invented by marketing executives as part of their mission to mangle the language.

It's a rule that, although English has served most of us pretty well since Shakespeare's day, it isn't quite good enough for the marketing world, which prefers to make up its own words or borrow French ones or – and this is the favourite - make up words which sound French.

I particularly admire the L'Oreal Plenitude Activ-Futur range, which probably does all three and pioneers a new marketing technique – if you want to make a word sound really exciting, just lose the final letter.

This is an advance on the usual attempts by the marketers to sound chic and French by, for example changing 'clinic' (which, along with 'gusset' is one of the least glamorous words in the English language) to Clinique.

One popular marketing ploy is to preface the product's name with 'le' written in upward-sloping script and sometimes coloured bright yellow to indicate that 'le' is a really sexy, happening word, unlike 'the' which is a just a definite article.

It is perhaps not surprising that the worst offences against linguistic common sense, including Vivality, come from the cosmetics and toiletries industries, whose products, being mainly jazzed-up soap and grease, need all the help they can get. And next time you feel yourself falling for the marketing and believing that shampoo can really make you vital and vivacious, remember that this stuff doesn't come from London, Milan and Rome, as it says on the bottle, but from, for example, an industrial estate in Slough.

Cool for cats

Say my name is Rory and I'm pretending to be a leading marketing executive.

The task I've set myself is to make Whiskas cat food sexy and inviting, even though it's composed of mushed-up bits of animals, some of which, I should think, would disgust even a fairground burger-bar owner.

At present Whiskas, like most cat food, is sold either in gravy or in jelly. Cats, even though they shouldn't have any say in the matter unless they are prepared to make a contribution to the family budget which, since the dawn of time, they haven't been, have very firm opinions on this. They like either one or the other and drive their owners mad if their owners get it wrong. So where, to outflank the cats and open new opportunities in the cat food market do we go from here?

34

Whiskas in sauce bearnaise? Whiskas with beurre blanc? Whiskas in raspberry coulais?

No. Rory says that there are cost implications and actually the best thing to do would be to launch a third type of Whiskas with neither gravy nor jelly. While everybody in the brainstorming session gasps and falls over backwards, Rory delivers his coup de salesmanship. "We'll call it Country Pate", he says. "Brilliant!" they all agree. And it's now in the shops, making life a third more difficult for cat-owners, or, which is the same thing, cat feeders.

In contrast the worst piece of marketing I've seen this week is for a radio-controlled atomic watch accurate to something like half a second in a thousand years. "Never be late again!" is the slogan.

If I was worried about being late, I wouldn't touch the watch because nobody is ever late because their watch is not ludicrously over-accurate. They are late because the traffic is bad or they'd been daydreaming or (most commonly in my case) they've got slack standards.

Knowing, to a nanosecond, exactly how late you are has never been of any use to anybody.

Mashed Swedes

Ikea and casinos (and I'm thinking here of the prairie-sized slot machine floors of Las Vegas casinos) are other worlds; they exist quite separately from the streets we live in. There are no windows, no weather, no sense of time and in both (I think, though my memory of Las Vegas casinos is hazy) there are no distracting music or jingles advertising special deals to recall you to life. Human voices are muffled and buried by the immense surroundings, and your fellow shoppers or gamblers seem tormented souls fixed on one idea and condemned to pursue it to eternity, or at least until they can find the exit, which is more or less the same thing.

Occasionally you have to kick yourself to realise that you are not in some circle of hell, you're in Birstall, near Leeds, so pull yourself together.

But I still can't help worrying, every time I visit Ikea, that I may have been captured by a weird Scandinavian cult. Cult members must only eat Swedish food, they must understand Swedish screw sizes, they must, as a test, be able to pronounce the names of the many Ikea product lines which, although Ikea is a global company, only make sense to Scandinavians (Liding, Utby, Hovskr, or Grundtal for example).

They are instructed that if they follow the Ikea path righteously, they may one day be connected to the Great Soul, which takes the earthly form of a giant meatball.

Oh dear, I think I may be becoming unhinged, which is generally what happens when I enter large shops. I did warn my partner Lynne but she said we needed a new kitchen and this was the place to go.

She was right of course; I have to say that Ikea, despite its sinister cult overtones, sells a comprehensive range of solidly-built, stylish furniture at affordable prices and I worship at its altar (altars in hard-wearing beech laminate being available from £7.50).

My only complaint, apart from having to lug all your purchases around even though you didn't sign on as a warehouseman, is that Ikea kitchens are fitted with mixer taps only.

I've thought and thought about this and can see no advantages at all in mixer taps and don't know why they make them. True, they are half as likely to break down as separate taps but if the mixer tap breaks, you're in twice as much trouble.

The great disadvantage of mixer taps is that the pipes are constantly contaminated by hot water so it's impossible to get really cold, refreshing water unless you run the mixer tap for ages or spend lots of money on special fridges or water coolers... oh, now I get it.

Absolute zero

Fantastic news! This week I discovered the QVC TV shopping channel! It's changed my life!

QVC is available ABSOLUTELY FREE with a simple set-top digital box. That's right, ABSO-LUTELY FREE and that means you won't have to pay a single penny. Ever.

Ah, I hear you asking, what do you get for that? Well, you get hours and hours of repetitive, vap-id, badly-presented banal sales drivel which at first drives you into a spitting fury but, if you lis-

ten to it for long enough, becomes strangely relaxing and zen-like.

Its secret, as a kind of mind enema and medita-
tion aid, is its relentless emptiness. You could
listen to QVC for days without being reminded
of anything unpleasant or complicated from the
real world. The repetitiveness becomes hypnotic
and reassuring, like a hot bath where the water
never runs out or turns cold.

Also QVC doesn't sell high-tech products likely
to leave you feeling inadequate and confused. I
really do try and keep up but I don't, to be honest, fully understand anything at the Comet su-
perstore apart from the toasters and some of the
more obvious white goods.

But this is no problem at QVC, where time has
somehow stopped in the world of the 1970s and
80s TV soap Crossroads. The male presenters all
have that handsome, chiselled, well-groomed,
sorry-I'm-a-bit-thick look of doctors on daytime
TV soaps, or, if you can remember that far back,
magazine editors on another soap, Compact.

The studio decor is low-rent Dallas and the female presenters are predominantly blonde, engag-
ing and enthusiastic, so you think that, had they
not been totally obsessed by shopping, they could
have made a career on Blue Peter or even
Newsnight.

However, they prefer spending hours of their
time presenting the most gloriously daft and
pointless programme on free digital TV – Shades
of Diamonique.

Diamonique (which is probably popular among shoppers who think Clinique is a very classy name) specialises in selling 'replica' gemstones.

For instance, if you had to buy a five-carat, emerald-cut diamond pendant in a diamond shop, it would cost hundreds of thousands of pounds. In QVC you can get exactly the same thing, except it's not a diamond, for less than £40. And what makes this offer really special is you can also buy the Diamonique pendant in pink or green, which real diamonds don't stretch to.

My QVC-watching afternoon also included an hour-long feature on a home gym which looked like an ironing board and on which three blonde ladies had to disport themselves in supposedly interesting ways. The sheer mindlessness of it was the equivalent of three Prozac tablets, all absolutely free.

Clas of its own

For Christmas 2011, I bought my partner Lynne a digital meat thermometer.

This was because it was on offer at Clas Ohlsen, the strange Swedish shop whose speciality is selling things it's difficult to think of a use for.

Also it was shop-closing time on Christmas Eve, which is when I buy all my Christmas presents because it concentrates my mind, even though it can lead to inexplicable buying decisions.

Which explains the digital meat thermometer, which I didn't even buy batteries for because I didn't think anybody would ever use it — I mean why, unless you were Heston Blumenthal or an idiot who couldn't follow cooking instructions, would you?

Anyway this week, I realised that the thermometer had gone over a year without being taken out of its box and was very unlikely to ever get used, so the best thing would be get rid of it in a creative and sustainable way.

But how?

I think it only cost about a fiver, so it's hardly worth putting on eBay and a charity shop might regard it more as a puzzlement than a selling opportunity.

Giving it to a poor person, who could only dream of owning a lump of meat big enough to take the temperature of, would be grossly insensitive, so I think I'll just leave it on a bus and let it take its chances – and this year's most useless Christmas present, a spiritual head massager made of wire that's more scratchy than relaxing and would only be of use if you caught head lice, may have go to the same way.

This reluctance to throw things in the bin is probably connected to my 1950s childhood, when any electrical implement, even the simplest food mixer, seemed fabulously exotic and when people expected everything to last for years and years.

That's why I've still got a video player underneath my TV, even though it's not connected to anything and I've put all my videos in an inaccessible corner of the loft, where I hope they'll be unearthed by someone who will find their covers amusing, like old knitting patterns. The important thing is, nothing must go to waste.

SIX

Thinks…

Here are some thought pieces, although I prefer to talk about things rather than thoughts. I think, in retrospect, I should have been kinder to the Olympic games.

Cross purposes

So tell me this; if capitalism is the only way of doing business, how come collaborative crossword solving gets such good results?

It's generally agreed that competition is the engine of growth, which I'm sure is generally true, although so much of British business – the utilities, transport and privatised firms doing public-sector tasks, – are not really subject to free-market disciplines because they're cartels, which is to say a device for fleecing the public, and they've got, as their one customer, the state, which, according to enthusiasts for naked capitalism, is a sump of ineptitude, so why do they think out-sourcing a sump is the answer to our problems?

But let that lie and let's get back to collaborative crosswords. These are things I've done all my life –well, since sixth form, when me and my tearaway mates formed the Daily Telegraph Crossword Crew, mainly because the Daily Telegraph was delivered free to the school.

The rock-hard Telegraph Crew had to spend hours and hours trying to finish crosswords because we were only 17 or 18 and cryptic crossword-solving is one of the very few skills which, like afternoon naps, get easier the older you are.

And after that, I established crossword-solving relationships with all sorts of people. It's a bit, I should think, like ballroom dancing – you can do it competitively but really it's better done as a conspiracy to make all the dancers, including yourself, look better than they are. Paintballing sessions, I'm told, sometimes end up as conspiracies too, in which decent, collaborative people turn on unpleasant competitive types who take daft team-building exercises seriously.

Every year, on some Saturday in spring, I return to a marvellous house in north Wales where there's an annual all-day – and most of the night – garden party for an extended network of very old friends and their children and their children's children.

On party day, we always have two or three copies of the Guardian prize crossword laid out across the garden tables, because many of us are Guardian types, which is to say we like being mildly left-wing and drinking alcohol.

Our main activities are idle chat and solving the crossword in a rather slack manner because nobody wants to be the top crossword-solver – in fact having a top crossword solver, who could do the puzzle in 10 minutes, would spoil all our fun.

It's like when I used to play badminton with my children.

We are not a sportingly-gifted family, so rather than allowing players to slam the shuttlecock down and leave opponents feeling humiliatingly defeated and cursed by a life-sapping inferiority complex, we made it the object of the game to keep the shuttlecock in the air for as long as possible by collaborating not to fire fierce shots which could not be returned.

This did a lot (though actually not enough) for the family's levels of hand-eye coordination and healthy exercise because the non-competitive form of badminton can last for hours and hours.

There was a time when almost every day there was a made-up story in the popular press about some loony left-wing school abolishing competitive sports days.

I think competitive athletes should compete to the highest levels; the rest of us should just find a level we're comfortable with.

It would improve the mental and physical health of the nation no end if everybody didn't have to be a winner.

Puritanism reinvented

Turn it down, stub it out, pour it down the sink and please ensure you are doing all this while respectably dressed – the new puritans are taking over.

Correct that – the renewed puritans are taking over. Britain, when not drunk or going through one of its silly phases, such as during the pantomime season, is a puritan country, much like, and for the same reasons, the United States.

It was the US that invented Prohibition, which, being largely ineffective and a huge encouragement to big crime, set puritanism back several decades.

It took even longer than it should have done for puritanism to re-establish itself because the post-Prohibition world was interrupted by the Second World War and it's hard to maintain anti-smoking, anti-drinking, anti-sex values while expecting people to die for their country.

But things progress, so that although at one time it was thought acceptable for sailors on Atlantic convoys to risk their lives so that stressed-out wartime citizens could smoke Virginia tobacco, we now realise that, by modern standards, they were in fact Dealing in Death and should have been (as is the puritan way) frowned upon.

My own attitude to renewed puritanism is ambiguous; for example, I no longer smoke or approve of smoking but I think you should be kind to smokers, who live within the law and probably contribute more to the general-taxation pile than I do.

And although, according to my libertarian values, I should approve of people who like me drink more alcohol than is good for them – I can see there is an unarguable case for cutting back a bit.

It's just that the anti-alcohol campaign seems to be a rather vicious extension of the anti-tobacco campaign; we've got the smokers on the run, the puritans seem to say, now let's start on the drinkers.

Not that the campaigners would ever say they were campaigning. Just look at the cost of drinking in terms of broken health, shortened lives, reduced working efficiency, violence and accidents, they say in that annoying more-in-sorrow-than-in-anger tone.

And anyway, I don't think the campaigns against smoking and drinking are the worst aspects of the puritan resurgence. That would be the campaign against children.

Children, we learn from the puritan press, which is the popular national press, are dangerous things in constant danger of eating themselves to death or attracting paedophiles. Watch them like hawks, cover them up and please don't laugh at their silly jokes.

Bad banking

I spent about 20 minutes in a bank queue this week waiting to do a very simple transaction while the lone counter clerk tried desperately to sell the bank's financial products to each customer in turn.

It was a bit like being badgered by a hustler outside a Third World airport – well, with several obvious differences but in the sense that the young woman had clearly been trained not to take 'no' for an answer and would have liked to have shouted out 'Hey mister, this is your lucky day, I can make you rich, rich, rich' if only the regulatory authorities hadn't recently clamped down on that sort of thing.

One man told her he didn't really want an exciting new ISA because he was only visiting and would be going back to China next week. "Our ISAs can be accessed from anywhere in the world and offer an excellent rate of return by international standards," the bank woman responded, skilfully glossing over the fact that an excellent rate of return by international standards wouldn't currently buy you a teacake.

The man mumbled something and rushed out with his head down, knowing that it's best not to show hustlers any sign of interest or you'll never be rid of them.

The next customer, a sensible teenage girl student, paid a cheque in then had to explain that no, she didn't want a savings account because she had to live on £40 a week and had no savings and no, she didn't want a credit card because she wouldn't trust herself with one, even though the bank said she could have a lovely card with a funky modern design and a CD voucher tomorrow.

Then the bank woman played her last card and the student had to say that no, she didn't want the bank's special deal on mobile phones because, er, she hadn't got a mobile phone. It had exploded last week. And then fallen into a pond, and she wouldn't be getting a new one ever so could she go now please?

And the moral is? Firstly, the banks shouldn't pester honest people into becoming liars; secondly they shouldn't turn the speech amplifiers on their counters full-on so everybody can hear your private business, and thirdly they should redeploy some of their staff from telephone cold-calling sales tasks, so that every bank has at least two counter clerks on duty at lunchtimes.

Oh, and fourthly they should stop calling the counter clerks or tellers fancy names like 'customer advisors' and, as they used to do when banks were responsible institutions and not a national joke, they should employ solid middle-aged people, often called Sheila, Jean, Jim or Colin, who have no sales responsibilities but are very friendly and highly skilled at handling money, that being very much their point.

(Afternote: This was from 2008, though I don't suppose the banks have learned much since).

Take a break

I have a friend who works at Leeds University and he found that the university's administrative efficiency and creativity fell like a brick when staff started working through their lunch breaks and eating sandwiches at their desks.

This is because macho managerialist culture cuts out essential forums for what my friend calls 'horizontal communication', such as the pub, cafe or canteen, where information goes across and around rather than laboriously up and down, or more often just down and out, never to be seen again.

The point is that organisations such as Leeds University, the NHS and whoever it is you work for, assuming it's not a kebab shop, are increasingly laden with too many managers holding meetings lasting far too long because they've outlawed the simpler, money-saving device of getting responsible, professional people to talk things through in their own time and at their own expense.

It will be interesting to see how bloated managerialism survives the downturn; I don't see how the NHS and big corporations will be able to react quickly enough but the kebab shops will probably sail through.

Incidentally, I like the phrase 'horizontal communication' on the grounds that it sounds rather filthy if you've got a mind like a sewer.

Playing schools
Universities are going, in terms of recruitment and funding, through tough times.

Which is a pity, because education is the one thing (well, excepting polo, cycling, rowing and dressage for a start) that the British are good at, even though, for entirely political reasons, we have to agree that ordinary, local authority schools are utterly useless.

Otherwise there would be no point in constantly reorganising them so as to satisfy the vanity of ministers who want to educate children in their own image – and obviously I'm looking at Michael Gove here, although a succession of Labour education secretaries were no less vainglorious because it's a job that allows you to play head teacher to the nation, just as becoming a health minister allows you to play doctors and nurses. Gosh, they must think, this is a lot better than doing the jobs we're fit for – which, in modern politics, means mostly policy advisor, PR person, consultant or some other post of no obvious use to the world.

The thing is that the government doesn't want to shout about its achievements because that would mean giving credit to people who do proper jobs. It's fairly sure, however you count it, that children are getting better results and that crime has been going down over the last ten years, so wouldn't you think that ministers would like to take personal credit for that, while, as an afterthought, mumbling, not too loudly, some thank-you words to the teachers, police, probation officers, council staff and other public servants who actually brought about this very encouraging trend?

Well no...because how can government ministers (including David Cameron) make a great show of being tough on crime when, assuming the whole point of the exercise is fewer crimes, the professionals have already got there.

In education, where the policy seems to be that a policy more than a week old is in need of a shake-up, politicians have decided that former soldiers might be better at teaching children than teachers are. This may be because, having no specific and useful skills themselves, the politicians can't distinguish between teaching and soldiering, or between lesson plans and ballistics, although I'm sure teachers and soldiers (and even small children) could.

Anyway, I think things have come to the point where people who love their careers in the public service should realise that governments will do everything in their power to make life difficult, so their best course, from a job-satisfaction point of view, would be to move some of their energies into the voluntary sector.

In education, this could mean teachers and lecturers moving back not to the 1950s – Michael Gove's favourite decade – but to the 1850s, when, in mechanics' halls and temperance institutes across the land, recently-literate workers were listening to enlightening lectures and lapping up knowledge without the need to collect certificates or enter a career path. They just enjoyed the novelty of being told about things.

Now, with high unemployment, and even higher part-time employment, it could be time for a return to this kind of earnest, old-fashioned approach to education.

Obviously, it would be hard to justify on cost grounds, but since so many people have so much time on their hands, wouldn't it be good for everyone if, through a programme of public lectures, teachers could ignore pompous, misguided ministers and remember their purpose, which is to inspire and inform the ignorant.

Misplaced passions
Of course, all sensible people dislike the phrase: 'We're passionate about…' because it's likely to be followed by something ludicrous, like 'intelligent roofing solutions' or 'holidays in Northamptonshire' or 'guinea pig hygiene'.

But I think it goes further than that; the idea that you should be passionate about many things other than love, politics, science or art is inherently dodgy and possibly unBritish.

I mean, any old supermarket or restaurant will claim to be passionate about food, but can you imagine the very sensible Delia Smith salivating wildly and able to speak only in grunts over her recipe for macaroni cheese? What to have for tea is an interesting and important question; it should not, in a sane and balanced world, have anything to do with passion.

Sport, of course, is something that people get very worked up about – but not as worked up as newspapers or broadcasters. I remember walking through a huge crowd of football fans in Leeds just after England had been knocked out of the World Cup by Germany.

The next morning's papers explained that this was England's Day of Agony and that the whole nation was in mourning, which came as a surprise to me because I couldn't see any fans, even the ones wrapped in England flags, who appeared

52

more than mildly upset and let down by the defeat.

I think there must be a streak of common sense in the English character which cautions against investing too much passion in the fortunes of the national football team; nobody, except maybe a few over-excited football commentators, believes that, having beaten the mighty Wales 1-0 this week, England will go on to bestride the European football championships like a colossus, although making it past the quarter-finals would be rather nice.

Then we'll have the Olympics, an occasion – because it gets worse every time – for unprecedented hype and a few great clashes in the athletics stadium, but otherwise just people doing games.

Of course I'm not being dismissive of the great effort and dedication put in by Greco-Roman wrestlers, fencers, archers or others; it's just that I find it difficult to get worked up about other people's hobbies and although I'll be very pleased if the Brits win the lightweight double sculls, I think tears of joy shed by anybody but the competitors themselves would be seriously misplaced and possibly unhinged.

And I've just remembered that I said earlier that it was OK to be passionate about politics. Now I'm not so sure, because Col Gaddafi made violently passionate speeches and look where it got him, whereas John Major made sensible, understated speeches and…well, as Ron Moody sang in Oliver!, I think I better think it out again.

SEVEN

Local knowledge

I live in Woodhouse, an inner-city suburb of Leeds, which has council estates, semis, streets of red-brick, back-to-back houses, interesting people, lots of students and a neglected park. Read all about it…

All's right at the pub
> *The lark's on the wing,*
> *The snail's on the thorn,*
> *God's in his heaven*
> *all's right with the world.*

That was Robert Browning (1812-89) celebrating the reopening of the Chemic Tavern in Woodhouse, even though he didn't know it at the time and in my view went completely over the top.

For a start, I've never seen a lark in Woodhouse, in inner-city Leeds, although I've seen quite a lot of police helicopters, and secondly the Chemic Tavern is only a pub and had only been closed a couple of weeks, so why bring God into it?

I reported exclusively from the front line last week on how the pub's unexplained closure had left many of the regulars severely traumatised and had reduced the area round the Chemic into a

54

wasteland of lost, wandering souls – but, although there may have been several hospitalisations, nobody actually died. This wasn't the relief of Mafeking or the Berlin air lift.

Still, the closure was not a simple affair, it was preceded by a long period during which the pub seemed to be slowly bleeding to death.

Every day another beer ran out and was not replaced, leaving the regulars staring blankly at the pumps, bemused and broken.

It was a truly pathetic sight and possibly, to be fair to Browning, worth a few lines of poetry.

But now The Chemic is back together again, sparkling clean and bright and under charming new hosts who seem determined to understand and cater for the needs of Woodhouse folk (pubs that sell beer, for a start).

The reopening did restore some sense of normality, continuity and identity to the area the Chemic serves – and in a big, sprawling city you need a local focus, or at least a local.

The focus would once have been St Mark's Church, which still stands on top of its hill looking down on everything but is now just a pile of stones; its congregation sadly decamped and its graveyard a disgraceful mess.

So The Chemic has to carry a lot of responsibility; it is an institution. Everybody knows that a village without a pub is only a collection of houses and the old, solid, four square Chemic creates its own village around it, so long as it's got some beer and customers in. Which is probably why those lines of Browning came straight into my head as I walked for the first time through the Chemic's reopened doors...my village was back and the lark, in a metaphorical sort of way, could not unreasonably be said to be on the wing again.

A lively life

My friend Ruth (who sometimes goes under her Afro-Caribbean name of Root, although she's not Afro-Caribbean, just in favour of interesting variations) is the landlady of the Chemic Tavern in Woodhouse, Leeds.

She says that once, when she was even more young and foolish than she is now, she painted a friend, a victim of an alcohol-induced collapse, with clown make-up then went to sleep herself. He woke up completely unawares, walked to the nearest chip shop and, without realising he was a clown, ordered a fish supper. This was in Lincolnshire in the 1980s when such things didn't happen often.

She's since caught up with him.

He went on to become a professional model for a leather biker-gear magazine and got engaged to one of the Three Degrees.

Ruth's view is that this proves that some people lead more interesting lives than others. We tried, in the bar, to improve on that but really there's nothing more to be said.

Negative vibes

A friend of mine, in the front line of the war

against halfwits, told me, at an essential after-work relaxation session at the Chemic Tavern in Woodhouse, Leeds, of an Anti-Social Behaviour Order which got subverted by an unfortunate grammatical error.

The Asbo conditions said words to the effect that the named person must NOT:

• Not swear and spit and people in the street.

• Not scream like a banshee for no reason.

• Not wear clothing that makes decent people want to vomit.

• Not make funny faces at guide dogs.

Which, meant, grammatically speaking, that the poor young man could only be arrested if he forgot himself and accidentally behaved peaceably for a moment. Fortunately, having spent hardly any time at school, he had no idea what a double negative was so justice was upheld. This proves that Lynne Truss and the grammar and punctuation pedant's isn't always right.

A mess to cherish

This week, as is my democratic duty, although I've never thought to exercise it before, I telephoned one of my local councillors to demand what was going on.

"What's going on?" I demanded and Coun Penny Ewens, clearly used to dealing with deranged electors, wondered politely whether I might be referring to plans to graft a car park on to a proper, and very important, Leeds park, Woodhouse Moor.

And although I'm mainly interested in the Woodhouse Moor question because it is, broadly speaking, in My Back Yard, I think it also raises more general questions about how cities like Leeds can continue to be pleasant places with population densities approaching those of downtown Kowloon's and not many more planning regulations than a Brazilian shantytown.

Coun Ewens is an admirable and energetic councillor. She is also, unlike me, entirely in favour of the Woodhouse Moor car park, which means, though I'm not one to pick fights, I will have to argue with her. The proposed car-park site is between the moor's magnificent monument to Queen Victoria and a collection of tawdry takeaway shops.

It's in a grassed area also containing a statue to the forgotten industrialist HR Marsden plus, if you're in luck, a man walking his dog or a crow head-butting the rock-hard, not-exactly verdant ground.

(It struck me, walking home from work across the moor yesterday, that it would be a good idea to do a quick chisel-and-plinth job and change HR Marsden into Charles Dickens. I mean, they look pretty much the same and driving past Charles Dickens would be a lot more uplifting than driving past HR Marsden).

A collection of committed community groups is fighting to save the moor, but I don't think anybody has so far argued the case for spare and useless land being left spare and useless as a matter of policy.

If the bit of scraggy grassland around HR Marsden's statue were to be used sensibly, there would be scarcely anywhere in central Leeds not dedicated entirely to cars, flats, offices, flat-letting agencies or more flats.

Coun Ewens says the car park's surface could be made of something softer than Tarmac, but it will still have to have white lines and pay-and-display machines and will, I'm sure, look so much like a car park that nobody will mistake it for a moor.

The area will also be landscaped. One of the glories of the threatened piece of moor is that no landscaper has laid hands on it. The dandelions grow wherever they like and the trees around the edge are essentially big weeds; all over the place, chaotic, in need of a trim and somehow loveable.

I think they are more in keeping with the anarchic, fairground spirit of the place (it's next to the site of the old Woodhouse feasts) than the straight, bobble-topped artist's-impression sort of trees landscaping will bring. And the worst loss will be of what planning officers call visual amenity. This isn't just me; so many people have said that there is something special about walking from Leeds city centre and coming, at the top of the moor, across a huge green vista with church steeples and enormous trees in the background and no parking machines in sight.

And I've thought of another very good argument against tidying up Woodhouse Moor. Somewhere

59

in the middle of it there is a large and unplanned puddle and, for a few glorious days a couple of weeks ago, a pair of mallards moved into it.

Their whole scheme was misconceived. They would not have been fed, as they would have been in the far posher Roundhay Park, on best quality bread; they would have had to eat old kebabs and left-over chips. And there would have been drunks and druggies to deal with and, worse, ornithologists because this is a university area and it would have been very difficult to have any kind of sex-life (which, it being spring, was probably a priority) without somebody taking notes.

What really ruined it, though, was that the puddle was a bit too shallow for the ducks to swim in, so that although they looked quite serine when floating, as soon as they tried to move they started stumbling about like Norman Wisdom and looking extremely undignified, even for ducks.

So I don't blame them for moving on but that doesn't affect the principle that puddleducks and feral trees are things to be encouraged. Down with car parks, up with untidiness.

Afterword: The car park plan was called off following an energetic campaign by local people.

Shades of Yorkshire

This week, I visited an international evening at Quarry Bank primary school in Woodhouse, Leeds, where the children come in all shades and from many backgrounds, although most of them speak fluent Yorkshire.

You would have had great trouble organising an international evening at my primary school in north Lincolnshire in the 1950s.

This was almost entirely white and English, exceptions being a few Americans left over from the war and the staff of the town's solitary Chinese restaurant, where, as all the children knew, the fried rice was really fried maggots.

At Quarry Mount school there was international food ranging from curries to that multi-ethnic favourite, mini Cornish pasties. In fifties Lincolnshire, you would have had difficulty finding an olive and I'm not sure that kiwi fruit had yet been invented. Children did sometimes eat food containing garlic, but only as a dare.

The Quarry Bank evening included very exciting Asian drumming from a large group of pupils of many backgrounds, which I suppose could stand as a kind of clunky metaphor for the success of the school's ethnic mix (different children, same beat…get it?)

There was also Irish jiggy music and polkas and a group of black and mixed-race boys in front of me responded particularly enthusiastically to the Irish fiddling. I found this rather puzzling until I recalled that, the way things have got mixed up since the fifties, the boys could well have been Irish.

I can only remember one song from my Church of England primary school, a missionary hymn which I hope no longer exists in any hymn book. It started, as I recall (probably wrongly):

> *Over the sea there are little brown children,*
> *Mothers and fathers and babies too,*
> *They have not heard of their Father in Heaven*
> *No one has told them that God is true…*

We had to imagine the little brown children of course, never having seen one, and we were never told that they might have had their own religions, the world being split, it was thought, into Christians (preferably C of E) and savages.

And in case you think I'm being nostalgic about those innocent pre-PC days, forget it. They were awful, ignorant and dull and I'm sure that if I had spent my primary school years at Quarry Mount, I would have learned more and certainly had more fun.

Quarry Mount, the most imposing, even beautiful, school in Leeds, looks down over back-to-back Victorian terraces and across a dip to the equally imposing Anglican church of St Mark's, closed about 10 years ago but due to be restored and reopened under new Christian management.

Looking down from the windows of the school hall, it occurred to me that if one of the hell-fire St Mark's preachers who attempted to keep the ragged Woodhouse flock in line were to return to the streets of today, he might at first think not much had changed. He would need to enter the school to realise that nearly everything has – and for the better.

EIGHT

Prominent people

I can't do celebrities. I know no famous people and can't even recognise them when they're on the front page of Hallo magazine, so you'll have to do with these.

Professor Vanessa

I've decided that you should never make a joke in case it comes true.

Not that this was a joke, just a piece of innocent flippancy. I was writing, about a year ago, about Dr Vanessa Toulmin, who, raised in a Lancashire fairground family and born on tour, turned legit by entering academia and eventually became the director of the National Fairground Archive at Sheffield University, which I often call upon as a source of fascinating photographs when… well, when my column needs to be enlivened by a fascinating photograph.

Her remit also includes sideshows, circuses, novelty acts and freaks, which makes her one of my heroines, rather like Mariella Frostrup, although obviously for different reasons and can we get back to the subject please?

I wrote back then that I hoped Dr Toulmin didn't rise to become a professor because, given her variety background, the words 'Professor Toulmin' would naturally be followed by something like 'and her dancing chickens.'

And guess what happened next (or as we say nowadays, guess what happened going forward)? Well, Dr Toulmin hasn't only become a real certified professor ain't she? (and I apologise for my inability to handle Cockney double negatives, I'm from Lincolnshire).

This promotion is a thoroughly good thing; it's just that I worry that Prof Toulmin, who last month organised a Blackpool freak and sideshow event, complete with a headless lady, might find herself taken less seriously than, say, a professor of Anglo-Saxon literature, although obviously a lot more seriously than an emeritus professor of finance and banking.

Incidentally, I understand that the highlight of the headless lady show came when the showman invited a member of the audience to test the knee-jerk reflex of the lady, who everyone assumed to be a waxwork. When the lady's leg shot forward, there were screams and fainting-fits all round.

And talking of dancing chickens and similar things, which we sort of were, my friend Claire and her mates went to the Chemic Tavern in Woodhouse, Leeds, at the weekend dressed in dungarees and straw hats because they were on their way to a country-and-western hoedown evening.

To the right of them were half a dozen rather gloomy mime-artist clowns (at least I think that's what they were – you don't like to ask mime artists) and on the other side an eccentrically-dressed group who, according to the consensus, although the consensus couldn't be sure, were probably – who knows why? – having a chicken impersonation contest.

Claire, in her fake ginger plaits and felt-tip freckles, was glad when it came time to move on. She was concerned that, if things had gone any further, they might have started to get silly.

To the slaughter

I find it obvious that Prince Charles can fairly be described as mildly fascist if you agree that the classic elements of fascism include a misty attraction to national myths, a deference towards the rich, violence of expression and weird clothes.

On the first point, I would refer you to the very misty, sub-Wagnerian pantomime surrounding the installation of Charles as Prince of Wales in 1969, which even I, as a callow teenager at the time, could recognise as a prime example of what his more sensible sister would have called appalling naffness.

(Oh, but the British do pomp and ceremony so very well, everybody says. No we don't, it's pantomimes, the Boat Race and darts we do very well).

65

Not only that, the ceremony took place at Caernarfon Castle, built by Edward I during his crushing of the Welsh nation and the real princes of Wales, and would have appeared a very crass choice of venue were you to credit the Windsors with any kind of ethnic sensitivity.

Which you can't because both the Prince and his very English Duchess like hanging around, as if it's part of their heritage, in tartan kilts, which are for Scottish tribesmen or drunkards, or anybody who enjoys wearing them but they do not hang well on members of the Saxe-Coburg and Gotha family who, even in a mongrel nation, are about as far from the Celtic fringes as you can get, which, geographically and coincidentally, is probably the Windsor area.

Prince Charles, for all his half-cocked New Ageism and his admirable (which is a word I'm using just to appear fair-minded) seriousness, really does have that fascist tendency to extremism, so that, for example, he doesn't want to cull or control grey squirrels, which originate from north America; he says he wants to eradicate them – the lot.

The idea is based on the belief that 'alien greys', as he calls them in an attempt to strike horror into our hearts, are threatening the native red squirrels and it is quite unhinged. Are ordinary, fair-minded urban Britons likely to watch calmly as ruthless marksmen blast amusing grey squirrels from their bird tables; will not children feel obliged to start a petition to the Prime Minister when the stench of torched squirrel reaches them in their local park?

Prince Charles has the backing of his trade union, the Country Land and Business Association (CLA), on this. The association says that squirrels (along with deer, although the Prince doesn't want these to be eliminated because then what would we shoot?) are devaluing its woodland assets by millions because they strip bark from trees.

Which might be true but slaughter and cruelty are so obviously bad things that the interests of the Country Land and Business Association and Prince Charles shouldn't be able to override them in a civilized, humane, urban country. That would be rule by the rural rich.

Incidentally, red squirrels, abundant in continental Europe, are not by any measure an endangered species, although I suppose that might change if grey squirrels continue to move west, but I'll set that aside for the moment because I don't want to spoil my argument.

In fact, it's only British red squirrels that are at present under pressure and they, of course, are not a zoological species at all but a Beatrix Potter, Squirrel Nutkin cultural construct laden with misty ideological nationalist undertones, rather like Prince Charles.

Big Mary

On Sunday I watched a short play about a big life – that of Mary Gawthorpe, also known (which

67

gave the play its title) as The Woman from Woodhouse.

Mary was a teacher, trade union official, orator, free-thinker, suffragette and trouble-maker. She was small ("bird like" according to one description) but she must have had the voice of a she-elephant because in 1908 she addressed a crowd of 250,000 at a suffragette rally in Hyde Park, London, and she also spoke at huge rallies across the north of England – including one on Woodhouse Moor, Leeds, in June 1908 which drew 100,000 people.

I think they only fitted in the park because as well as being more politically engaged, people were thinner in those days.

The rally must have pleased her very much because she was born just round the corner from the moor, in Melville Street in 1881, the daughter – like many working class Woodhouse Victorians – of a leather worker.

She qualified as a teacher through on-the-job training and night-time study because the family couldn't possibly afford to send her to college.

Her mother, who would have liked to have been a teacher herself, was clearly very supportive of her clever daughter and the relationship is touchingly displayed in The Woman from Woodhouse.

The play can't do full justice to a woman who was born under W.E. Gladstone and died, 92 years later, in the era of Mick Jagger. But this Theatre of the Dales production, written by David Robertson and directed by Jennifer Jordan, is, as is

68

typical of the company's output, very fast-paced and economically sustainable – just three very good actresses play all parts (including the crowd scenes) and manage to the convey a rich period in Britain's political history, when people could be bothered to try to change things.

Mary entered politics through her friendship with Tom Garrs, a member of the Independent Labour Party and a compositor on that hotbed of revolutionary socialism, the Yorkshire Post.

She met Cristobel Pankhurst and other leaders of the suffragette movement – who I wrongly imagined, before hearing Mary's story, were all imperious middle-class blue-stockings – and became a full-time organiser for the Women's Social and Political Union.

This involved numerous arrests, a two-month prison sentence, forced-feeding and several beatings-up, including one in 1909 when she heckled a speech by Winston Churchill. By 1912 her health was broken but she still helped to establish a journal, The Freewoman, which advocated free love and sexual liberation and was described by one suffragette supporter as "indecent, immoral and filthy."

What is odd was that this woman, who created so many disturbances and made so many enemies, looks, on photographs, as gentle as a dove. Sylvia Pankhurst described her as "a winsome merry creature with bright hair and laughing, merry eyes" and "having so sparkling a fund of repartee that she held dumb with astonishment vast

crowds of big, slow-thinking workmen."
In 1916, her health recovered, she moved to America, where she became an organiser for the garment workers' union, married – typically keeping her maiden name – and died in Long Island, a very long way from Woodhouse, in 1973

Sceptical about sex

This week [note to readers – the week of Margaret Thatcher's death], when it seemed everybody was talking about the same thing and nobody could get very far without using the words 'conviction' or 'belief', I escaped to the sanity of the pub – specifically the splendid Victoria Hotel behind Leeds Town Hall.

Here I attended a meeting of the discussion forum Skeptics in the Pub (their 'k', not mine) and nobody mentioned Margaret Thatcher because they were all far too busy talking about sex.

The speaker was Dr Brooke Magnanti, who, to fund her Sheffield university doctorate in forensic pathology, worked for some time as a high-class call girl, or, which I think means the same thing, an expensive prostitute.

She wrote a hugely successful blog about her experiences under the web-name Belle De Jour and a book and a TV series, starring Billie Piper, followed.

Brooke Magnanti doesn't look very much like Billie Piper but shares, despite being born in Florida, her natural-blonde, wholesome appeal. Perhaps living in a small village in the Scottish

Highlands, as she does now, has frozen the Florida girl out of her.

She is also charming, good-humoured and, particularly relevant to this pub visit, a natural sceptic, meaning she feels obliged to question accepted beliefs and fads, in this case those surrounding sex and gender. The view that men are from Mars and women are from Venus can be dismissed on any number of grounds, she says, not least the feet-on-the-ground, eminently sceptical one that both men and women are from Earth, obviously.

Her book The Sex Myth deals with the mass of confusion and misrepresentation surrounding sexual politics. In particular she analyses the recent invention of alleged disorders such as sex addiction and female sexual disfunction (known as FSD to make it seem more scientific), which are good business for therapists, counsellors and the pharmaceutical industry but of limited use to anyone else.

The pattern is that somebody comes up with an alarming study showing there are huge numbers of people in need of treatment for sexual disfunction, then the study slips unquestioned on to the internet and gets referred to so often by lazy journalists that it develops enough critical mass to become both an accepted fact and a small industry.

Meanwhile, amid all the fuss, the fairly rare people whose lives are made a misery by their sexual problems get overlooked. If you take it to be a sign of FSD that sometimes women don't really fancy sex, you'll produce more heat than light – more headlines than sensible diagnoses.

Incidentally, Brooke Magnanti recalled that when she was about to marry, her husband-to-be, who knew of her career in the sex trade, thought it would be good if they both admitted how many sexual partners they had had, so as to get things off to an honest start.

She hadn't kept count but thought maybe 500, taking the total rapidly down to 300 when she noticed the shocked look on his face. He said four – although, after thinking hard all night, he decided he could possibly make a case for five. Which led her, perhaps drawing on her professional interest in statistics, to a strange and rather haunting quote from Josef Stalin: "Quantity has a quality all of its own." This could, I suppose, be true both of sexual scorecards and counting the victims of the Soviet terror.

Death by water

On a freezing evening in Leeds last week, by the banks of the River Aire and next to the Asda supermarket headquarters, I, along with scores of shivering people, the Lord Mayor of Leeds and the Assistant Chief Constable of West Yorkshire, paid tribute to a hopeless loser called David Oluwale.

Mr Oluwale, although I don't think he was often addressed as 'Mr', was a vagrant with psychiatric problems who had to wait until a few decades after his dreadful death to attract the interest of people with titles and epaulettes.

He would have vanished unnoticed if he hadn't become, in Leeds at least, a cause celebre because of the kindness of decent people who know an injustice when they see one.

His story is bleak. In 1949 he arrived in Hull as a stowaway on a ship from Lagos, Nigeria, moved to Leeds, got a job, married and had two children. Then, in 1953, he was given a 28-day prison sentence following a raid on a nightclub and his life went to pieces.

The process was described in a film shown at the event on the spot, beside the River Aire, where David Oluwale was last seen alive.

It included, among other things, Leeds Nigerians remembering their countryman, including one who arrived in England as a stowaway at about the same time as Oluwale and went on to work for more than 40 years at the now deceased metal works, Kirkstall Forge. Life-paths can turn out differently.

Poor David, though, fell into a terrible pit. From being a lively and sociable man, he turned, after several years in an asylum, into a wreck who couldn't, one of his friends remembered, make eye-contact with anyone.

Then the police, and two of them in particular, started persecuting him, dragging him out of shop doorways to give him regular, cruel beatings until April 1969, when he was seen running away from them towards the river Aire.

His body was fished up two weeks later and, although a manslaughter charge failed, his two police tormentors were eventually jailed for assault, which for the time, was a heck of a result.

The tribute event was extraordinarily poignant, partly because the weather was freezing so we were thinking about a street-sleeper while appreciating how very cold streets can get, and partly because we were beside the river and there were beautiful images of the Aire on screen – David Oluwale, we remembered, arrived in Yorkshire by water and left by it too.

As well as the big-wigs, there were wonderful performances by a street-theatre group and poetic children. The chairman for the evening took about half an hour to thank all the people who had helped to compile the tribute, which itself was quite a tribute to a hopeless loser.

NINE

Party animals

Most of the party-related incidents described here are entirely true, although, to quote Mark Twain, some have been stretched. I think amuse-bouches have now gone out of fashion. Good.

Frottage forbidden

Yes, the planning stage of my summer garden party is going splendidly, and thank you for asking.

I realise that you may be worried by my track record and I see your point; the statistics do look poor – three parties organised over four years and, even if you count them, as I prefer to, as one glorious rolling event, the guest list still only totals nine.

But that was a learning process. This time, believe me, I'm getting it right. For a start, I've started distributing my very stylish invitations already – a full six weeks before the event.

If there is one thing I've learned, it's that if you leave the invitations for a party until the afternoon of the day before, people will think up all sorts of prior commitments and moan about not being given enough notice. This way, they've got no excuse for not rearranging their holidays, funerals, baptisms, weddings and medical appointments.

There is, of course, a danger that if you go for the six-week option, those same party-poopers will pretend they received their invitations so long ago, they forgot about them.

I'm working on the theory that the ideal invitation time may lie somewhere between six weeks and half a day, so, for my subsequent parties, I will gradually narrow the gap until I get into double figures on the guest front. I'll keep you posted.

Meanwhile, I intend to have the best of both worlds by reinforcing my early invitations with an intensive leafleting campaign the afternoon before, probably outside the Town Hall.

The quality of the invitations is also important. In the modern party world, it is no longer acceptable to draw a crude map of where you live, scrawl 'party tomorrow' above it, then photocopy it until the paper runs out.

The invitations this time have been prepared in the knowledge that today's more discerning party guest wants to know exactly what's on offer.

I have therefore included on my invitations a pithy, bullet-point summary of the party's attractions, including my fully-upholstered deckchair, the availability of toilet facilities and the fact that my house is on a major ambulance route.

I've also told a bit of a fib, which, in the competitive party market of the 21st century, is, I think, accepted by potential guests as almost inevitable. I've said that there will be a frottage area – frottage being an indecent and lascivious rubbing-together of bodies which, although it will attract a certain kind of punter, I would not want to happen in my garden.

So I've roped off the frottage area and, come the day, will hang a sign over it saying 'Frottage Area Closed' which will stop them in their filthy tracks. I don't think they can sue either because, if the railway companies can cancel their advertised trains at a moment's notice, it must, I will tell the court, be legal for me to cancel my frottage area.

The invitations also point out that, due to the prohibitive cost of stylish invitations and frottage signs, guests may have to bring their own food, drink, chairs, music and, come to that guests.

Spoilsport Sally

My annual summer garden party has, at the last minute, taken a new turn. It will now, and for the first time ever, celebrate healthy living and pure thoughts.

I've been struggling to come up with a mission statement to express this exciting new development and am at the moment choosing between 'Delivering wholesomeness,' 'Fun with responsibility' and 'No drunks.'

All this has come about because yet another beautiful young woman has come to stay at my house. First it was Claire the ballet dancer (as explained in the Oliver Cross column No. 373, although I don't suppose you've kept the cutting) and now it's Sally the medical science student and frankly it's wearing me down.

I mean, it's nice to have bright, friendly, long-legged blondes running round my house but I don't know how many more of them I can take. All that eating salad and drinking fruit juice and watching my language is taking its toll and I hope I don't snap and go on a rampage of depravity, leaving coffee-mug rings on the table, wearing odd socks, eating kebabs and being rude to lettuces.

Sally has become my lodger because she is working in a lab at Leeds University over the summer and her mum, an old friend of mine, reckons having Sally there will keep me out of mischief and give me a more mature attitude to life.

In fact, Sally's mother's ploy has worked well. For the first time ever, I've created a life-improvement plan and introduced firm rules and guidelines into the household so that both Sally and I know where we stand.

It took some negotiating but so far we've agreed that

1) I will only smoke in the garden

2) I will only smirk in the garden, and this applies to all unnecessary facial expressions and noises because this is not Blackpool Pleasure Beach, is it?

3) I was not born in a barn

4) You would have to be a complete idiot to go

the expense of buying a refrigerator and then leaving the milk to turn sour on the kitchen windowsill, wouldn't I?

5) Pot Noodles are poisonous

In return, Sally has agreed to drop her demand that I go jogging with her on Woodhouse Moor first thing every morning, so long as I produce a medical certificate within the next two weeks.

Actually, I'm making Sally out to be a bit frightening, which she isn't at all. She's lovely, it's just that modern young women can be a bit daunting to people whose sloppy values were formed in the 1960s and 70s.

For example, my friend Lynne, a right-on feminist in her youth, now finds her daughter working at the Playboy clothing shop and wearing the Bunny logo which at one point she would probably have set fire to, although she can't do anything about it now because kids need jobs .

Anyway, my garden party will now take its cue from Sally and be thoroughly sensible and well-behaved. Unless (Plan 2) I can get her to start on the vodka, in which case we go back to Square One.

A moo's bouche

The centrepiece of the food spread at my 2006 annual garden party was a wax-covered cheese cow produced by the Wisconsin dairy board.

I find it astonishing that the country which produced Edison, the Model-T Ford and moon rockets could also invent the Wisconsin cow. I mean if you were at all worried by the prospect of the world's only superpower bossing us all into submission, look at the Wisconsin cow and feel reassured.

Not only does it look as dumb and inept as Keith Chegwin and as unthreatening as Judith Chalmers, it's also got a primitive, vulnerable, wonderfully crass quality which makes you want to hug it rather than eat it. As well as the cheese cow the Wisconsin tourist board also presented me, on a press trip to the Great Lakes, with a wax-covered cheese in the exact shape of Wisconsin.

This, I thought, was a very inspiring marketing idea and I would have made it the garden-party centrepiece if I had thought it at all possible that any of the guests would have had any idea what Wisconsin was shaped like and wouldn't have concluded they were looking at an oblong of cheese with bits missing due to rodent infestation.

Also, the State of Wisconsin cheese underwent a mild explosion in the aeroplane hold on the way back and I decided, after eating some of the bits, that it really wasn't worth reshaping; it's a truth that good, strong cheese is a wonderful thing and that additive-packed, industrialised, artificially coloured cheese should only be fed to rats or people you don't like.

Which didn't stop me offering my Wisconsin cow to the guests as an amuse-bouche ('amusement for the mouth'), which is a little delicacy such as a braised pigeon's tongue stuffed with marinated wild truffles and mixed-fruit jam given away free to diners as a way of justifying the absurd prices charged in the sort of pretentious, cliche-ridden restaurants which serve amuse-bouches.

I realise, of course, that the Wisconsin cow is not a delicacy, it's a big, stupid cow, and that none of my guests would recognise an amuse-bouche even if they ate it in error while seeking out their favourite party food, which is generally Cheesy Wotsits.

But the point is that I tried; I can't bring sophisticated eating to Woodhouse, Leeds, all by myself. All I can try and do is raise the tone a little.

Generally, my garden party went very well so long as you ignore the word 'garden'. Since it was pouring down, most of the action took place in the house and thank heavens that, due to the rain and my inherent unpopularity, my small lounge and dining room didn't get overcrowded. Also the poor weather cut down on the riff-raff, although only to a certain extent. Lynne put on a great spread and I gathered, from feedback from my damp guests, that I had done my bit by bringing along the Wisconsin cow, which everybody agreed was one of the most amusing articles of foodstuff they had ever seen at one of my parties.

Colour of trouble
Lynne has thought of a theme for my annual summer garden party which may be hard to beat

81

(and I'm sorry if you've just come in, but thinking of themes for my garden party is a continuing concern of this column and my partner Lynne is better at it than me.)

She thinks we should go for red, mainly, I think, because she has found a recipe for tomato and beetroot curry with red peppers, which, served in cochineal with tomato sauce and geranium flowers, would be so definitively red that even my guests would (for once) have an inkling of what the party was about.

She also thinks (being hopelessly optimistic and not knowing my guests as well as I do) that everybody will be able to find dashing or subtle touches of red to enliven their outfits.

My prediction is that, rather than picking out clever red accessories, the guests, forever prone to overstatement and drama, will either empty tins of red paint over their heads or scream loudly so as to reveal their engorged tonsils or self-harm with Stanley knives or, most likely, forget the theme entirely.

The other worry is that red is the colour of violence - bull fights, for example, or Casualty. This is a shame because red, like all the primary colours, is vibrant and life-enhancing and far preferable to the calming, boring beige I chose, on police advice, as the theme colour for my 2003 garden party.

But red has this very important upside: Our local New Labour MP, Hilary Benn, might, as a conscientious representative, feel obliged to call in on my very popular garden party just to show how cool and in touch with local feelings he is. We don't really want him to because, quite frankly, hardly anybody around here lives according to New Labour values; I mean, eating low-fat guacamole dip and discussing The Way Forward For a Better Britain isn't our idea of fun. But if we all dress up in red so as to look like crazed socialists, I think Mr Benn will leave quite quickly and we can all get back to normal.

Great leap forward

As I write (although not necessarily as you read), the weather is so sunny and warm that I would be tempted to use the word 'glorious' if I didn't have a resistance to clichés or sounding like a cricket commentator.

It's made me think that I should perhaps revive my legendary summer garden parties, which I may have mentioned once or twice.

Not that they were legendary in a good sense – it's more that there are confused and conflicting accounts of what happened at the parties and some people, clearly easily traumatised, have chosen to deny that they took place at all.

But I've been looking through the cuttings and much of it is coming back to me, including a defining moment in which a goldfish jumped out of my garden pond and landed on top of a big Alsatian dog, which left the dog thoroughly confused and caused some of the guests to wrongly conclude that they had been hallucinating.

Each party had a theme – one of the most successful being 'beige' in which guests were encouraged to wear beige cardigans, eat beige food (notably the insides of Cornish pasties) and speak in an uninspiring, beige sort of way. They managed the last task very well, but then they did that every year.

If I were to hold a garden party this summer, I suppose the theme would have to be 'austerity', because gone are the days when generous party hosts could throw money away on unlimited Pringles and budget lager.

I think there would be a difficulty in relaxing the dress code, standards being rather low to start with, but perhaps there could be a prize (probably, as in past party competitions, a never-yet-claimed toast rack) for the guest wearing the most frugal outfit – or, to raise the bar slightly, the most frugal outfit recovered from a skip.

It's a little late to start making my own wine or brewing my own beer, but perhaps I could rustle up an austerity punch using own-brand soda water, a bottle of blue Wkd left over from Christmas and a tin of fruit cocktail, if they still make it (and if they do, I'll extract the cherry before distributing the punch – these are tough and selfish times).

Canapés, or snacks as we used to call them before an unsustainable boom gave us all big ideas, might be a problem, but I might look into starting a temporary food bank.

Me and my partner Lynne (who I've not yet told

about my garden-party revival ideas in case she faints) are going to a themed garden party in Wales later this month, and the theme is France.

I did toy for a moment with the idea of wearing a beret and striped jumper and putting a string of onions round my neck, but then remembered that the party will be so full of brilliant and original thinkers that somebody else might have had the same idea as me.

Going as Louis XIV was rejected on cost grounds and I haven't really got the physique for Zinedine Zidane.

So I'll be dressing as a generic French philosopher in the Jean Paul Sartre-mode. It's dead easy – roll-neck black sweater, thick black glasses, half-smoked Gauloise or pipe in the mouth and a thoughtful expression in the eyes. I think the impression will work best if I remember to say nothing at all to anybody.

French dressing
A couple of weeks ago, I was having a crisis over what to wear to a French-themed garden party in Wales.

As I explained, I didn't really want to wear a striped jersey and beret or hang a string of onions round my neck because I thought somebody else might have the same idea. As it turned out, nearly all the guests did, the more imaginative of them adding a home-made Poirot moustache, although I don't think Poirot sold French onions, possibly because he was a Belgian

There is, though, a slight connection between Wales and French onion-sellers because I was once told that French onion-sellers (who existed in large numbers when I was young) came mainly from Brittany and enjoyed selling in Wales because the Breton language is similar to Welsh and when you're from a small minority, it must be refreshing to find someone who knows roughly what you're on about.

Not that most of the guests could speak Welsh beyond a few phrases and some drink-fuelled songs, the party being in the English-speaking North Wales borderlands. Actually, despite the theme of the party, they couldn't speak French either, unless French is talking loudly in an Inspector Clouseau accent and saying 'zut alors' at random intervals.

But when you've been the victims of centuries of national stereotyping ('Taffy was a Welshman, Taffy was a thief'), it must be good to get your own back. Getting it back at the expense of the English would be even better but I suppose at an Anglo-Welsh party that might have raised tensions to Balkan levels, and one sure way to get all Britons working in unison is to make fun of the French. It's at least forgivable, although not wise, to mock nations and groups powerful enough to defend themselves – bankers, for example, though not, as happens all the time in the right-wing press, poorer people.

Plus, stereotyped French people are, as all Britons know, among the funniest beings on earth and can't they bring back 'Allo 'Allo, I say.

Anyway, the only party guests to get beyond onion-seller costumes were a woman who wore, quite against all my previous experience of her, a classically smart dress to express French chic (I don't think many people got it); a man who redesignated his bowling referee's coat as a smock, made a palette out of cardboard and couldn't remember whether he was supposed to be Monet or Manet. Plus me.

My original idea had been to wear thick, horn-rimmed glasses (available from the pound shop) and pretend to be Jean-Paul Satre, but I abandoned it on the ground that I didn't think I could maintain a Jean-Paul Satre level of conversation for more than about a minute, particularly while doing a dodgy French accent.

So, at the suggestion of my friend Jill, I bought a very cheap T-shirt and a permanent marker pen, consulted Google and created a shirt covered in interesting French quotations. There was wisdom from top thinkers including Sartre, Zola, Balzac, Rousseau, Voltaire ('I hate women because they always know where things are') and Eric Cantona. But the quote that created the most interest was from Edith Piaf: 'The whole of your personality is in your nose'. Almost everybody thought the best response to this was to grab hold of their noses in alarm and then to look pensive.

Tights in the fruit bowl
I had a day off this week when I could have done

all sorts of | interesting and self-improving things, but instead had to paint my downstairs woodwork.

This is because, much to my own surprise and at very short notice, I've arranged to hold a party this weekend which will probably involve some women tutting round my house.

They will go: Tut, he's let his dishcloths get out of hand; tut, there's a smear on this glass; tut, when did he last clean his skirting boards? tut, where's his Toilet Duck?

And what I have had to do is to paint my interior woodwork fresh brilliant white to divert them and stop them also saying, tut, he's smoking too much and that's why his whole house is yellow. What annoys me the most is that the biggest tuts will come from women who keep their old tights in the fruit bowl, whose fridges are a disgrace and who have never cleaned their oven even once, while I'm on my third clean in only five years.

It's not their messiness I object to, it's the way that feminism and the new relationships between the sexes have passed them by, so that they think a man living on his own must be in need of Doris Day. Even though the worst offenders are about my age, they remind me very much of my grandmother, born under Queen Victoria, whose constant refrain was that men, by their nature and without exception, were utterly useless and would fall to pieces entirely if it wasn't for female good sense and domestic skills (this was the grandmother who, as soon as they invented tights, threw hers straight into the fruit bowl).

That's why on a Radio 4 Women's Hour discussion, when one of the middle-aged panellists said as an aside that men never washed their socks, the other middle-aged women fell about laughing like they were listening to Tommy Cooper. The fact that the joke came from a lecturer in gender studies, who should really have been able to think of something a bit more cutting, wasn't the point. The point was that she was totally wrong and clearly hadn't been keeping up at all. If she had wandered through Leeds city centre on a Saturday night she would have noticed that the Turkish brothel-whiff enveloping the streets comes usually not from posses of half-clad lasses but from groups of freshly-showered lads. Men now have got far too clean and domestic for me, with their cosmetics, their health magazines, their new clothes and their fancy cooking; but their efforts have been completely wasted on the people who should have noticed, like lecturers in gender studies and two thirds of the middle-aged women who might just turn up at my party.

My own view is that a bit of messiness is fine and far more healthy than being too tidy because it protects you from obsessive cleaning disorder, which is more of a bother than the odd bout of salmonella. But I'm no more messy than most women born since 1950 and when they start tutting at me, I will point out that my woodwork is cleaner than theirs and pass them a fag to keep them quiet.

TEN

The end is nigh

Some people ask me whether a supposedly light-hearted (a word I hate) column should talk about death. Yes of course it should. It's celebrity news and moralising that drive me to despair.

A good death

You haven't seen me around for a while and neither have many other people. This means that I spend half my time bumping into people who say to me: "Haven't seen you around for a while - did you have a good Christmas?" At which point I have to brace myself for the answer: "Not really, my mum died."

Which I don't like saying because it's difficult for anybody under 80 (my mum was 84) to respond sensibly and naturally to death news. Mum had a leaky heart and decided that, since she was terminally ill, she would just like to die quietly, please, without medics and carers poking her around and, since she didn't like inconveniencing people, as quickly as possible.

The doctor came and said she should drink a thick liquid which contained all the nutrients she needed to prolong life. She told him he had missed the point and in any case the liquid tasted equally disgusting whether in banana or chocolate flavour and since she was dying anyway, couldn't she be let off drinking it?

To which the doctor had no answer and nor did my sister or brother or my partner Lynne, who had gathered around the bedside in a bid to buck her up but then realised that bucking-up isn't always appropriate or to be wished for.

A day after the death, one of my mum's elderly bridge club pals rang to ask how she was and I put on my dignified, funereal voice (I don't use it now...too tiring) and said she had unfortunately passed away. "What's unfortunate?" the pal said. "That was what she wanted, wasn't it?" Um, yes, but you have to be a bit older than me (which of course I will be before I know it) before you become so brutally accepting of death.

The good news about my mum's death was that it happened at home; both the actual moment and the process, which lasted maybe two or three weeks although, it being a fading away rather than a crisis, it's difficult to put a start to it.

If anybody wants to start a campaign for home deaths on the same basis as the campaign for home births I would be happy to join it – particularly as home births might carry a slightly increased risk of death or injury, whereas home deaths can't really make things worse.

The carers (highly-skilled, friendly, sensitive, vital in an ageing population and paid a lot less than compensation-claim salesmen) called round four times a day but the rest of the time she was in the bosom of her family. Which is an old-fashioned phrase because home deaths are old-fashioned. They don't, barring chip-pan fires, happen so often.

The family watched my mother die (no, it's not a release or an ascension, it's a failure of the pulse) unsurrounded by plastic curtains or nurses or orderlies gathering round with mops.

Really I'd love to phone my mum to tell her how well-handled her death was, plus lots of other interesting things, but I know, as my mum did better than me, what a logical impossibility is. She also taught me that sentimentality is to be avoided all costs.

End of a friend

On Sunday my friend and colleague Martin Woods died, not suddenly but very quickly, aged 44.

He would have died soon anyway, of galloping, untreatable lung cancer, but dying is a different thing from being dead, which pulls you up and makes you think – although not, in my case, in any profound way. I've just been thinking about what a lovely man Martin was.

After work on Monday, when we heard of the death, we went, by instinct, to the pub. There was nothing practical to be done; he, his very nice wife Lindsey and two young children were all in Ireland, which is where he comes from and where, in what he knew was a farewell tour, he had gone to visit his mother and relatives.

The plan, until Sunday, was that when he returned to England we would call round with a big bottle of Irish whiskey – we didn't want to just let him go.

I can't say the mood at the pub was sombre and we didn't do eulogies, although we did recount some of his escapades (he was a great one for escapades). Mostly though the chat was disjointed and aimless; everybody's mind was on the man who wasn't there.

As we left the pub we did something we never normally do, being a sceptical, unsentimental lot. We gave each other hugs.

I think this was in recognition that a common disaster had befallen us; it wasn't that we were worried about our own mortality or the unfairness of early death, it was just that we all liked Martin. It was, though, a totally useless gesture, a kind of tribute.

I can't do a proper obituary because there are huge areas of Martin's life I know nothing about and, if they were to do a seating plan at the funeral tea, I would be on table 14 and quite happy to be there, knowing that Martin had so many close friends and kin that table 14 would be no disgrace.

But I did work opposite him on our little corner of the features sub-editors' and designers' desk at the Yorkshire Evening Post for a long time and I do want to mourn him.

He was a lovely colleague, he did the job well and never moaned or played politics. He liked, though he got through an awful lot of sub-editing work, fun and games and singing songs (mournful opera tunes most of the time, The Campdown Races, all umpteen verses, when he was feeling boisterous).

It was only a small part of his life but it helped our little corner to get through the days very happily.

Also, though I saw him socially only rarely, I knew, through what must have amounted to hours and hours of amiable office chat, that he was a thoroughly good family man. He was always taking the kids to practices and events and he adored his family holidays.

He had what they call a big hinterland. He was an aficionado of opera and sport (especially boxing and even, which I thought strange in an Irishman, cricket); he was very well-read and wrote very well, covering Northern football for The Times newspaper and coming back with tales of grim games in Rotherham or Grimsby. (Knowing that I know little about football, he spared me the statistics and told me funny stories about the pies instead, which was kind).

He wrote a column for the Yorkshire Evening Post spin-off, Yorkshire Sport – it was called Mr Angry.

I don't think he ever was seriously angry, although he could do an excellent rant, but he did have a great ear for pretension and silliness.

I should have mentioned before that he was big in an expansive kind of way. Not fat but strapping – a generous six-footer who could never quite get his shirts or trousers to fit.

I once met his sister, a doctor over on a visit from Ireland, and was struck by the family resemblance. Not particularly in looks (you would have had to thin Martin down a bit and iron him thoroughly for that), but in the general impression of good-humour, charm and intelligence.

This is how generous he was: At one of my annual garden parties he decided to make everybody mint juleps. (He was a cocktail aficionado as well as a sports aficionado and one of the most bewildering and enjoyable nights of my life was when I trailed behind him as he searched the whole of Leeds for the perfect Vodka Martini. Martin didn't get drunk often but when he did, it was with great panache and thoroughness).

Anyway, he was disappointed that I didn't have an ice-crushing machine to make the juleps with (his house in York, which makes things more upsetting, is a lovely family home, all scrubbed and polished and busy and full of things like fish kettles so that he could, in his generous way, serve his guests whole salmon.)

His solution to the crushed-ice crisis was to wrap the ice cubes in a towel and bash them furiously with a house-brick on my dining room table, which caused some damage.

Still, it was a typically big and generous gesture and a very tiny chip so I never complained. I'm now glad that I've got something to remember him by.

Salute to super Ted
One of the overlooked drawbacks of living into your nineties is that you don't get many contemporaries at your funeral.

On the other hand, if you've used your years well, as the recently late Ted Garrett, 93, did, you can still have a very good send-off from lots family and friends of all ages.

Ted, former cobbler, corner-shop owner, soldier and prisoner of the Nazis (Hitler gave him a bar of chocolate on his birthday – Hitler's not Ted's) led a very good life, being generous-minded and interested in other people.

For example, he used to let my now-partner Lynne cash her post-dated cheques at his shop when she was a cash-strapped young nurse before, well, she became an older nurse.

And his funeral at Lawnswood crematorium, Leeds, was full of touching anecdotes; for example, taking his granddaughter to Lapland and delighting her by whooping around on a skidoo and getting lost in the woods aged about 80, or, with his wife, taking in a French exchange student decades ago and making her a lifetime friend, so that she wrote to say she would have been at Lawnswood if a volcano hadn't erupted in Iceland.

Which aren't very big things, but they are very good things of the sort seldom noted in the public prints.

I knew Ted only late in his life, when I moved to Woodhouse, Leeds, because his son, Terry, used to take him for a drink at the Chemic Tavern in Woodhouse, where I sometimes go, and many interesting conversations ensued, often involving people 50 or even 70 years younger than Ted.

(In my favourite exchange, Terry and Ted were bickering in a friendly father-and-son way when Terry said: "We're getting like Steptoe and Son" and Ted chimed back with: "Yes, but which one are you?").

So it was fitting, as we say with bowed heads and muffled voices, that in Ted's last journey to Lawnswood, the funeral cortege stopped not only at his former home, vacated very recently when he moved to a care home, but also at the Chemic Tavern, which was a poignant moment although, given the contrast between the solemnity of the cortege and the raggedness of the tavern, I couldn't help wanting to smile.

In chambers

This week, with the coming of spring and a growing sense of renewal and the call of B&Q, I found myself thinking of the Hal Saflieni Hypogeum, an underground city of the dead in Paola, Malta.

Which isn't as strange as it seems because visits to DIY stores do tend to get me down and the

97

hypogeum is more heartening than you would expect of a prehistoric burial site.

It is the oddest World Heritage Site I've seen. Because of the limited access, only 80 people a day can visit (you have to book well in advance), so there are no crowds around the entrance, which is a dull, badly-signed building in a suburban side-street and could just as well be a dental practice.

The site wasn't uncovered until 1902, when there was a great rush to make houses for workers at Valetta's expanding naval dockyards and builders laying foundations broke into a 6,000-year-old wonder of the world.

Which they immediately tried to cover up again, because if there's one thing a speculative builder doesn't need, it's interfering archaeologists slowing things down as if they had all the time in the world (which, in a sense, archaeologists do have).

Anyway, eventually the size and age of the hypogeum (a word usually confined to burial tombs but which seems to mean any underground structure older than a basement) became clear – and it is indeed an astonishing sight.

There are chambers upon chambers, some clever elaborations of natural caves, which were once stuffed full of corpses laid to rest in a kind of crouching or foetal position, although given the scale and complexity of the construction work going on around them, I don't think they would have found it restful.

The intention seems to have been to assure the dead that they had not just been shoved down a cave and forgotten. The chambers have imitation windows, grand columns supporting nothing and useless lintels carved (without any metal tools) above the doors – on some walls and ceilings you can still see, looking very fresh, the red ochre patterns used for decoration.

Approached from the 21st century, the place is not sombre at all. What you can see is great energy and skill and, in the small sculptures found scattered around the site and now, unfortunately for visitors, removed to museums, great humanity too.

A typical figure is of a woman with enormous hips, very fat arms and a tiny head resting comfortably on a couch. She looks very contented and not at all sad, let alone deceased.

ELEVEN

Cats rule

The cat Tassos died. Note that I'm the only journalist in Britain who writes about cats without resorting to soppy words like moggy, puss or feline friend. The only word for cat is cat.

A deal with the devil

Cats: Weird animals or what? Discuss with examples. Well, for example, mine is often unable to find cat food in his cat food bowl placed in the cat-feeding section of the kitchen floor.

Which is even stranger because he quite understands the concept of shopping; so that when I arrive home with two handfuls of Morrisons bags, he works himself into a frenzy of anticipation, believing that no sane human would ever go to the shops if it wasn't to buy cat food.

And if I want to stop his manic purrings and strange cries and unpack in peace, I must feed him first. This produces a double-frenzy, because he also understands the concept of tin openers and the sight of one produces the nearest thing to an orgasm a neutered tom is likely to experience.

But when the food finally reaches the bowl, his tail plummets and then one of the most perfectly-designed hunting machines in the natural word (says David Attenborough) looks flummoxed and hurt and I have to pick him up and shove his face into the food so that he knows where it is. In fact, cats do lots of dumb things which can only be remedied through human intervention.

They get stuck up trees and trapped in all sorts of places no sane animal would have entered in the first place, because they know the deal by which they live with people: We are contracted to feed, warm and rescue them under all circumstances, they are contracted to just walk around being cats.

Of course it's crazy that we spend more on food for a destructive and ungrateful animal than we do on the starving of Africa; but we don't have much choice. The cat race made, at some point, a pact with Beelzebub and the human race has been paying for it ever since.

Partly this is because evolution gave the cat, as a by-product of making it the perfect hunter, the perfect face for wheedling food and shelter out of humans.

We are programmed to respond to round heads and big eyes which can look forward and meet ours because they remind us of babies. Note how, in Tom and Jerry, Jerry doesn't look much like a mouse – the real creature having tiny eyes set on either side of its mean, snivelling rodent face – but Tom is not far removed from a life drawing of a real cat.

And so cats have built on their original and useful skill of catching mice and moved into the people-parasite business; they have become like the plumber who came to mend your washing machine but liked your biscuits so much, he decided to stay. For ever.

Masters of the garden

Many people have problems with cats eating their garden birds. I have a problem with garden birds eating my cats.

Well, metaphorically – but only just.

The magpies which, every year in spring and summer, devote themselves to comprehensively trashing my garden, have got alarmingly bolder. They've always sneaked into my Italianate loggia (yes, I know it looks exactly like a lean-to shed but that's what a loggia is, stupid) so they can pinch scraps from my two cats' feeding bowls.

But this year, they haven't bothered sneaking. They've been strutting around openly like thugs who know Asbos can't be legally enforced against birds. They take what they want, even when the cats are in the loggia ineffectually chasing flies, which is their hobby.

The older one of the two did, about 12 years ago, bring home a dead bird (which I assume must have had had a heart attack and landed in his mouth) but didn't know what to do with it. He seemed very alarmed that the bird was covered in feathers which made him sneeze, having previ-

102

ously assumed that everything edible, apart from flies, comes covered in foil packaging.

This is why he never thought to eat my now-departed kamikaze goldfish, which used to jump frequently out of my garden pond and lie on the ground gasping and writhing in an over-stated, melodramatic way until somebody rescued him. The cat would just look at the fish quite closely but never laid a paw on him. (I think he was worried that the fish might contain feathers).

The good thing about all this is that the cats, through the magpies' bullying, have at least got a taste of real life and the ruthlessly competitive harshness of nature.

I'm hoping, without much hope, that this will be character-building and will stop them being such utter drips.

The danger is that they will react to the magpie humiliation by going all macho and trying to catch creatures they regard as big and menacing, such as fledgling wrens.

I resisted for years the idea of putting up a bird table in my garden because I didn't think it would mix with the cats. I needn't have worried; house sparrows (yes, we've still got some), blackbirds and tits swan around fearlessly, like they are living in a St Francis of Assisi theme park.

I've tried to make them more risk-averse by screaming at them to get out of the way of the cats but generally they take no notice. Really, the only beings with any authority in the garden are Lynne when, very occasionally, she decides that things are getting Beyond a Joke and need to be Taken in Hand and, at all times, the magpies.

Top tactic
Before Christmas I compiled my comprehensive Christmas Gift Guide, in which I pointed out that all you really needed to do was buy your beloved an interesting hat.

I was scoffed at but I was right because I presented my partner Lynne on Christmas day with a top hat from a fancy-dress shop and inside it, because things turned out rather last-minute and I ran out of wrapping paper, I placed a voice-altering electronic megaphone.

Some people might have been worried by this but Lynne immediately saw the point of the combination.

If you've got to live with two smug, annoying cats, there's no better way of wiping the supercilious smiles off their faces than by shouting at them through a voice-altering megaphone while wearing an alarming top hat.

The cat and the rat
Cats didn't get where they are today by being trusting and cute, like soppy and (of course) endangered water voles.

When my two cats saw the new carpet, they approached it in cat fashion, assuming it was a plot. They pussyfooted on it, which means they walked on tiptoe, as if on an uncleared Cambodian minefield.

But, like rats, they are also bold and curious so after overcoming the imaginary explosives, the cats turned their minds, if that's the word, to thinking how they could take advantage of the new carpet and within minutes had recognised it as a claw-sharpening opportunity.

This must have pleased them because the great puzzle for cats is why humans should do anything at all which isn't to the direct advantage of cats. That's why, when you unpack the shopping, their faces range from boredom to disgust as you haul out the vegetables and cleansing products.

Rats have the same survivalist mistrust of new or apparently useless things, such as stair carpets, as cats.

There was a great scare once because it was thought that rats had become immune to rat poison. They hadn't but they had evolved to be cautious and pussyfooting about it, so that when they saw a particularly inviting new pile of food, especially when accompanied by a 'Caution – rat poison' sign, they simply didn't eat it.

So cats and rats, both empowered with a potent mix of caution and adventurousness, are worthy enemies and perhaps the only thing that might save the human race is that cats also have an extraordinary capacity for stupidity.

Tassos to the end

My aged cat Tassos, who I've been saying for the last three or four years is not long for this world, is growing more distressed and distressing.

105

He is as thin as can be despite being, according to the vet, in good nick for a 20-year-old.

Neither the vet nor I can tell whether he is also happy, which I think is a vital and often overlooked point when assessing the welfare of the elderly.

Relevant to the assessment is the fact that Tassos has always been a compulsively sociable and communicative cat – a born schmoozer.

It was his habit until quite recently to sit outside the front gate and make friendly, reassuring noises to passers-by.

Quite sane and unsentimental people used to say, as if reporting it as a fact: "I was talking to your cat the other day."

In Tolstoy's War and Peace, there is a character called Sonya, a poor relation living with a relatively prosperous family who is said to be cat-like because she attaches herself to the house rather than to the people living in it.

This behaviour is typical of cats, so I can understand Tolstoy's over-generalisation, which, does, however, indicate, that Tolstoy never met Tassos.

There are cats that attach themselves to places or to the nearest source of decent food (preferably Fortnum and Mason), but Tassos, very unusually, takes a close and intense interest in the human beings around him – so much so that you wish he would revert to being Rudyard Kipling's primal cat-that-walked-by-himself, so that all places were alike to him and he wouldn't keep pestering you to screaming point.

Tassos, like a Stasi police spy, wants to know what you are up to at all times, following you to the loft, the greenhouse or, particularly annoyingly, the toilet.

He resents particularly people sleeping and slipping out of his control, which shouldn't be a problem because cats are supposed to sleep about two thirds of the time, but Tassos, particularly in his dotage, seems hardly to sleep at all.

Since his kittenage, he's realised that it's possible to wake people up by knocking valued objects off shelves.

My daughter, when she was very small, had a collection of cute plaster mice arranged along the top of her wardrobe. If Tassos couldn't wake her by conventional means, such as licking her with his sandpaper tongue or sitting on her face, he would start knocking the mice off the wardrobe in a methodical, one-by-one fashion until the whole household was awake.

Then he would look very self-satisfied and ask to be fed, watered and groomed because if there's one thing a cat can't countenance, it's slacking on the part of the servants.

Now, though, Tassos has become a shadow of his younger self.

He still, if there are any humans awake and moving, thinks it essential to forestall them from doing anything not directly beneficial to cat welfare. He will sit on any book or newspaper humans are attempting to read, walk all over their computer keyboards and jump up to obscure their view of the TV.

Except that now, it's all done in a spasmodic, purposeless, obsessive way, so that he paces around ceaselessly in circles, knocks things over randomly and can't do what cats are supposed to be best at, which is sleeping anywhere, any table or any chair.

Tassos wakes in the night almost as often as a new baby, and either starts knocking things off the bedroom tables or, if we've locked him out, howling astonishingly loudly and resonantly for a thing of skin and bones with a ribcage like a washboard.

I'm quite sure he has some sort of dementia, achy bones and sensory impairments and if he were a horse, he would probably be put down. Usually he looks confused and depressed or angry at his inability to move with energy and grace, as cats should.

But he can still schmooze and purr and take pleasure in his chief treat, Morrisons prawns (for some reason no other brand will do and you can't fool him because he recognises Morrisons shopping bags by the logo, I presume).

So I don't know whether his longevity is overall a good or a bad thing. I do know, from my experience of humans as well as cats, that adopting longevity as an absolute target for the NHS is a thing which needs thinking twice about.

TWELVE

En route

Here are some travel pieces, with, I was surprised to find, reading back, a particular emphasis on bus transport. I'm pleased that I've avoided saying that any of the places I've visited 'nestles' anywhere.

Land of the rising chicken

INDONESIA is one of the four most populous countries in the world yet few people know much about it, so, having just returned from two weeks there, I have compiled this comprehensive and fact-packed eight-point guide:

1 You've never seen so many chickens; every garden, every verge, every scrap of grass has plump families of them pecking away and the whole country is awash with virtually free free-range eggs.

> *INDOFACT: Unfortunately, I failed to find any good egg recipes.*

2 You've also never seen so many bicycles. The whole population seems to spend half their lives puttering about on little scooters and push-bikes, carrying their goods and children with them and driving in such a slow and civilised way that the passengers have time to read or do their nails.

109

INDOFACT: I can confirm that it is possible to carry two small settees on a pushbike, and a 12ft carpet roll on a Honda 50.

3 Indonesians are generally tiny people, both in width and height, which is why they fit so well on motorbikes (a family of four on a Vespa is not an unusual sight).

INDOFACT: Any woman who grows above size 14 gets her own show on national television, probably.

4 The common language of Indonesia, based on Malayan, was invented in the 1920s as a way of unifying the hugely diverse people of the archipelago.

INDOFACT: Indonesian has very logical and easy-to-learn spelling and grammar systems and you should consider making it your language of choice if you have trouble with English.

5 The country's stage of development is about the equivalent of Spain's 25 years ago. Hot water, washing machines and fancy toiletries are quite rare, yet most people are immaculately clean and fresh-looking.

INDOFACT: If Britons tried to live under similar conditions, they would look like Mad Max II.

6 There are all sorts of glorious tropical fruits sold at every street corner but the Indonesians' favourite is called durian fruit and smells and looks like a body part.

INDOFOODFACTS: a, *Walls make durian fruit Cornettos for the Indonesian market and*

110

they taste like fish vomit; b, Over there, Colonel Sanders swaps his stetson for an Indonesian cap in November and wishes everybody a happy Ramadan, like he's keen on people fasting; c, Frogs are widely eaten with rice or noodles. Don't believe anybody who tells you they taste just like chicken.

7 Indonesians are extremely polite and useless at expressing anger.

INDOFACT: Indonesian taxi drivers never swear and if they have to sound their horns, they go toot.

8 Garuda Indonesian Airlines has smoking sections on long-haul flights. The favourite local cigarettes are made with cloves and produce a clean and healthy feeling in your mouth, even though the World Health Organisation classifies them as very dangerous.

INDOFACT: Clove cigarettes make very inexpensive and unusual gifts for yours smoking friends, although it would probably be wise to get them to sign a cancer-liability waiver first.

The land Starbucks forgot

THE size of London makes me nervous. I know everything is supposed to be relative but London is absolutely big. It's the definition of big.

People promoting Leeds like to draw parallels with London but they don't work. Briggate is not Oxford Street however many times they say it is; the Leeds waterfront is not the London Docklands (which include docks big enough to drown

Otley) and York Road, although quite frightening enough, is not the South Circular.

The South Circular was actually the scene of a great triumph during my London trip. I crossed it – and not at the lights either. Of course I was terrified, but, as I always say to cheer myself up when doing something reckless and potentially lethal, like eating a pork pie, you could always get run over by a bus tomorrow, couldn't you?

Actually, there is very little point in crossing the South Circular except for the thrill of it. It runs, roars and splutters through the vast suburban deserts of South London and, where I did my dare, is exactly the same on one side as the other – an infinity of 1930s semis, every one of them worth about £400,000 and nearly every one with a Merc or a BMW in the drive.

(It's a wonder, though, how shabby the South London shops are, with a Costcutter and grubby curry house on every parade).

I was in Lee, London SE12, where my good friend Liz lives. I'm glad she was there to guide and encourage me across roads because, of course London is perfectly understandable if you live there – which I used to about 30 years ago, when I must have been bolder, because I don't remember being so scared then. It didn't help that the south London accent seems to have grown harsh and self-assertive, a parody of the accent I remember.

(I have no idea what Londoners speak like north of the river, where all shops, pubs and coffee bars appear to be staffed by a strange tribe of what could be Bosnians, who probably live in the drains because I don't see how they could afford regular homes).

Liz introduced me to a London that was new to me. Everything seemed done-up or improved. The Greenwich Maritime Museum and the National Portrait Gallery were extended and gleaming, the river was clean and the industrial Armageddon that was the Docklands was... well actually, it still looks a mess because it's not finished yet, but you can see it's on its way up.

At the Portrait Gallery I saw the original of Branwell Bronte's much-reproduced painting of his sisters. You need to see it in the flesh (not that Branwell could do flesh) to experience the poignancy of short and wasted lives. I enjoyed the Tudor portraits best – such clever, scheming faces, although they can't have been that clever because so many of them lost their heads (and if you were worried about losing your head, would you draw attention to your neck by wearing a big white ruff? I know I wouldn't).

Other highlights included a trip to China Town in Soho, which was of course bigger than any provincial China Town could ever be. I went into a Chinese pub thinking it might be an experience and found thick, thick smoke, great dinginess and, emerging from the fog, piercing Chinese sounds nearly as alarming as South London vowels.

It reminded me of an opium den, which sounds

racist but was actually my romantic side coming out. We had earlier travelled through Limehouse, which I like to imagine in its hectic Victorian heyday, full of Lascars and lightermen and pubs, ships and opium dens, rather than half-built flats and offices.

Greenwich Maritime Museum is impressive, although I thought the most remarkable museum piece I saw on my London expedition was Lewisham town centre.

I knew it 30 years ago and it didn't seem to have changed at all. Some of the net-curtained ladies' hairdressing salons and Formica-tabled coffee bars had probably not had a lick of paint since I last saw them, shabbiness being the south London way.

Probably, if you are one of those people who get sniffy about the Americanisation of British culture, you would be better moving to South London than the Hebrides, South London being the land that Starbucks forgot. Liz didn't ask me for my overall view of London, probably because I was looking a bit stressed.

(Afternote: This was written in 2001, when £400,000 was one of the biggest house prices I could imagine).

Encounter with an oligarch

ON Saturday, I attended one of the most important official openings south eastern Europe has seen for, oh, I don't know how long.

No really, I don't. This was in Armenia, a small

114

country of which I, at least, knew little, but the event was certainly big.

I was on a press trip to mark the inauguration of "the world's longest reversible aerial tramway". I'm not sure what 'reversible' means in this context but it is what the officials present, including the President of Armenia and the world-wide leader, called the Catholicos, of the Armenian Church, said was a catalysing development.

This means a tourism development so spectacular that it changes the game (oops, I've gone all corporate) and attracts other developments around it – the Guggenheim gallery in Bilbao being a good example.

The aerial tramway, which I would call a cable car but what do I know? is three-and-a-half miles long and rises to 320 metres through mountain and gorge scenery to the 9th century Tatev monastic complex, a great centre of learning in a beautiful green setting which was previously most easily reached by mountain goats, Armenian roads having their limitations.

This being a state occasion, the authorities were out in force. Police and army officers were in their most elaborate dress uniforms full of ribbons, epaulets and brightly-embroidered badges, like star members of the Brownies, and security men in shiny Romanian-style suits were slicking back their hair and indicating very firmly that they were not to be messed with.

There was also beautiful, stirring singing from Armenian priests' and women's choirs – maybe because that's what small, mountainous countries with inaccessible languages are good at, which would also explain Wales.

At one point during the opening ceremony local children released white doves – which have a huge resonance in Armenia because the country is the historical home of Mount Ararat, where, after establishing through spy-birds that the world was drying up, "God gave Moses the rainbow sign – no more floods, the fire next time."

The homing white doves, offered in many tourist areas overlooking Mount Ararat, are, I think, brought out so often that they can't really put their heart into it any more. The ones at the Tatev tramway opening made token flapping gestures before settling on the top of the stage and looking glum, a symbolic freedom flight of about seven-and-a-half feet, if that.

But the rainbow really delivered. At the point where the traditional Armenian dancing was about to start, a rainstorm hard enough to knock you sideways broke out, forcing everyone back into the hospitality tent, where it seemed right to enjoy some high-quality Armenian brandy as approved by Winston Churchill, who knew about such things.

We waited until the storm abated, not that we were in any rush, then peered outside to see the whole land looking bright and clean with a double rainbow ending at the Tatev tramway terminus, and if that isn't a good omen, I don't know what is.

The Tatev project was made possible through the support of a Ruben Vardanian, a billionaire Moscow investment banker who told me the tramway would probably never make money (particularly as local people could use it for free), but he felt obliged to support it, and a revival plan for the whole area, because "I'm an Armenian".

This is only a total explanation if you understand that Armenia, home to a very ancient Christian church and culture, at the crossroads between Orthodoxy and Islam, and scene of earthquakes and a shocking genocide, is quite unlike anywhere else, so that "I'm an Armenian" means a lot more than you would expect from a three-word phrase. Afternote: Mount Ararat, the symbol of Armenia, is actually now in Turkey because Comrade Lenin handed it over as a gift to Kemal Ataturk, even though a commemorative fountain pen would probably have done just as well without creating a continuing heap of resentment.

Ships to shores

Last week my partner Lynne and I had an exciting two-centre holiday, in Gosport, Hants, and Hartlepool, Teesside, and if you hang around long enough you will find an interesting connection between the two.

Gosport first. This is the Royal Navy town where my partner Lynne got her naval-nurse training, treated Earl Mountbatten for an unheroic condition and, on this visit, returned to a few of her

117

old, licensed haunts which didn't seem much modernised.

Next to Gosport, by ferry because this is a very ship-centred corner of the country, is Portsmouth, and Portsmouth Naval Dockyard, once one of the most important sites in Europe, now has a huge range of cafes, museums and visitor attractions but remains quite interesting for all that.

The star attraction, of course, is HMS Victory, especially the brass plaque marking the spot where Horatio Nelson (terrific name for a national hero – Nigel Nelson, for example, just wouldn't have worked, still less Des) fell mortally wounded.

On the same spot, very shortly before, the ship's clerk was literally shot in two and both halves were immediately shoved overboard; warships were bloody and ruthless places and, as I didn't fully realise before visiting the Victory, were so focused on killing that the guns were lovingly tended and given all the best berths, while the crew had to shove themselves into anywhere they could fit.

The headroom on the decks was severely limited not, as I thought, because people were shorter then but because the whole point of the exercise was to fit as many gun decks as possible into the ship – actually, the average height of a Victory seaman was, apparently, 5ft 7in and, although I don't know how they found anyone tall enough to measure him, the ship's carpenter was 6ft 6in.

Just along the quay from the Victory is HMS Warrior, launched in 1860 as the fastest, most advanced ship ever built; iron-clad, fully rigged for sailing and also powered by steam, armed to the teeth and, by comparison, making the Victory look like something you might play with in the bath.

But nobody remembers the Warrior because it never fired a shot in anger. This was when Britannia ruled the waves and all this super-ship had to do was sail (or steam) around looking dignified and important, so that ships from lesser nations either fled or sunk themselves out of nervousness.

And now let's fast-forward (although that wasn't quite the right word) up the M1 towards Hartlepool, where vessels from all over the word gathered for the climax of the Tall Ships Race.

You would need, as a son or daughter of a seafaring nation, a heart of stone not to be moved by all those ropes and sails and the poignant wood-on-wood creak of ships at anchor.

It's also a chance, rare I'd guess, to see Hartlepool en fete; the whole town seemed to be out and enjoying itself, with fairs, live entertainment, fireworks and stalls and inadequately-dressed local girls gathering to goggle at visiting sailors.

We walked for miles and miles, Hartlepool having a huge harbour area and all of it being fully utilized for the tall ships event, and at one point we came across a perfectly ordinary terraced house where an extended family had lit a barbe-

119

cue, put up awnings, and somehow kidnapped half-a-dozen Russian sailors, who looked terribly confused but, being used to northern ways, seemed to realise that it's senseless to quibble when there's booze and fags on offer.

And now, you might like to know about the connection between Portsmouth and Hartlepool, apart from the fact that they are both best avoided if you aren't charmed by outmoded ships serving no economic purpose.

Well, HMS Warrior, the terror of the oceans, ended up as a sad hulk used as a pontoon vessel for the oil industry until 1979, when a lunatic (I assume) millionaire paid to have it completely restored in Hartlepool.

This was a kind of last hurrah for all the Hartlepool ship-building skills which were then fading rapidly. The craftsmen did a magnificent job and in 1987 the ship returned to Portsmouth to continue its mission of looking dignified and important, rather like most of the royal family don't.

Life under the ocean wave

GOSPORT, Hants, is the home of the rather worrying Royal Navy Submarine Museum.

I've always been puzzled that anybody should choose to become a submariner; the plus points, apart from extraordinary comradeship, are that you are paid a bit more than an ordinary mariner and get to wear your own clothes when the sub is under water, but against this you have to live in a slum with the chance of being drowned.

I noticed, going round HMS Victory, that warships are essentially floating gun platforms; submarines are just floating guns, with torpedoes for bullets and the crew living in the barrel.

There is no room for showers or baths and personal space is so limited that the crew can't even take a full complement of socks and underpants – on a three-month voyage they apparently resort to turning them inside-out.

The genial ex-submariner who showed us around The Alliance, launched (or should that be sunk?) in 1947 and chief exhibit at the submarine museum, also remembered that the diesel engines produced a film of particles which were absorbed into the surface of the skin, so that you had to spend the early days of your leave scrubbing yourself clean rather than realising any fantasies which might have crossed your mind during the voyage.

I told him this sounded horrific. Oh no, he said, it was the time of his life. Stark staring bonkers.

Rich and poor

Guernsey in the Channel Islands looks rather like southern England until you notice odd details like blue pillar boxes, Norman-French place names, bank notes (including a £1 note) which can only be spent on the island and an impressive range of functioning public toilets.

Estate agents advertise quite ordinary houses for hundreds of thousands of pounds and most of the well-paid job vacancies are in banking and financial services.

But the impression of great prosperity is misleading because the housing market has two sectors, one 'open' and one restricted to people born on the island, and there are lots of islanders who don't habitually wear sharp suits because they work in fishing, shipping, farming, hotels and restaurants, building, waste disposal and all the other things a busy island needs as much as bankers and accountants.

Early on a Friday evening we found we couldn't fit into the most popular pub on the island's capital, St Peter Port, which was packed with the sort of end-of-the-working-week people you might find in a middle-market Wetherspoon's. The big attraction was, apparently, a free buffet.

So, despite a lot of big, posh cars – which can go no faster than 35mph, assuming they can move at all, the island's roads being narrow and frequently clogged-up – this is not Monte Carlo.

Which was the subject of a thundering editorial in the daily Guernsey Press and Star last week. This noted that around 40 local children (out of a total island population of 63,000) were suffering from physical neglect – meaning inadequate food and clothing - due to poverty.

The paper agrees that Guernsey is a fantastic place to bring up children "if you have money. If not, it is a particularly miserable place to be in relative or absolute poverty."

This, the editorial says, is a hidden problem because the island's decision-makers "do not rub shoulders with those for whom a half-million pound home, two cars and overseas holidays are not an aspiration but a daily, biting reminder of failure and isolation. No wonder the children suffer."

And the piece ends: "Perhaps the brutal truth is that this community of haves doesn't care about the have nots," which I don't think is the official view of the Guernsey tourism board.

Incidentally, the most sensible way to explore the island is by bus.

There are only two fares: £1 for all journeys, even those involving catching two or more buses, and nothing at all for the over-65s.

The drivers are polite and helpful and the passengers, when they board, smile and wave at everybody in a way which is rather alarming for mainlanders and suggests they've mistaken themselves for extras in The Wicker Man.

It is also possible to flag down buses between stops where it's safe to do so.

First Bus it isn't.

Africa by bus

I've just come back from 10 days in Senegal, West Africa, and therefore have very little idea of what Senegal, West Africa, is all about.

This is the glory of abroad; the way that foreign places, with layers upon layers of history quite outside your own, can leave you feeling gloriously ignorant and eager to learn. Not that I was starting from scratch. I was visiting my daughter Hannah, who has spent prolonged spells in West Africa studying migration, which also includes the endlessly-fascinating subject of how people get by.

Plus I had my Lonely Planet guide. Lonely Planet guides are great things but probably work better in small, tidy places like Luxembourg than in the great urban sprawl that is Senegal's capital, Dakar. You might think from the Lonely Planet guide that getting round Dakar would be pretty much like getting round, say, Coventry. But that fails to take into account the Africaness of it; the smells both worrying and intriguing, the crowds gathering in random clusters for no reason an outsider can understand, the Babel sounds of a multi-lingual, very vocal capital overlaid by the hooting of cars by drivers apparently intent on tearing to shreds the city ordinance banning the honking of horns.

Taxis are everywhere, private cars being in short supply, and in no case would a British MoT inspector begin to know where to start. Dials and knobs on the dashboard are represented by taped-over holes, tyres are generally bare, windscreens often broken. One driver, deciding to let some air into his sweltering cab, passed round his only window winder, keeping a very close eye on it, window winders evidently being like gold in the Senegal taxi trade. Still, the taxi system works safely and efficiently, the only problem, often a tedious one, being negotiating the price. This can be avoided by using the set-fare cars rapide, a near-miraculous form of mini-bus transport which, in my experience, takes you from wherever you are to wherever you want to go for virtually nothing and with no queues or hanging about.

The cars, brightly-painted and as ancient as the hills, carry 30 or more passengers with rows of three seats on each side and folding seats along the central aisle. Since the cars, being of a miraculous nature, are usually packed, a lot of manoeuvring is required to get on or off and the system depends for its success on an elaborate etiquette, with people for ever having to adjust themselves to let others through, always with a smile and a friendly 'Ca va' or whatever the Wolof equivalent is. The whole bus becomes a model of creative co-operation when it comes to collecting fares. Since the conductor, manning back doors generally held together by string, can't possibly pass along the bus, the fares and change get to their destination via many pairs of strange hands, with a smile at every hand-over.

Possibly more remarkable than all this was that the passengers, crammed in a rattling, rusty, overheated bus with a floor you could watch the road through, looked, in both senses, so very cool – the young working women in particular emerged from all that shaking-about with their immaculate hair and make-up and business suits intact, as if they had been delivered by air-conditioned limousine.

One form of transport the Senegalese don't go in for is baby buggies, the pavements being rough or non-existent and the kerbs unfriendly. The result, in child development terms, is that Senegalese toddlers, constantly hitched up within inches of their mother's heartbeat, are extremely well-adjusted.

They are also, probably because they are encouraged to get on their feet as soon as they become too heavy to carry, remarkably sturdy. If an African football team wins this World Cup or the one afterwards, I wouldn't be at all surprised.

Missing the buses

The bus network of Malta is astonishing. There are very cheap and regular buses to all parts of the small island with bus stops, bus stations and proper timetables – but the whole thing is built on creative individualism rather than any recognised public transport model.

Each bus is owned by its driver and the bus network is run by the drivers as a kind of workers' co-operative. This means that all the buses are painted in a corporate livery (orange in Malta, grey in the neighbouring island of Gozo) but, having been personalised by their owner/drivers, no two are at all alike.

They have makers' names – Leyland, Bedford, AEC, Plaxton and others – painted on them in bold lettering, which looks very odd; as if there was a time when British engineering was regarded as something to be proud of.

Many carry cheering, but sadly unrealistic, slogans on their bodywork – 'Sunshine for everybody!' 'Always be happy!' Generally they are more of in the spirit of fairground rides than public transportation units.

And of course, they can't last. The buses are in many cases ancient and have to pause for breath when going up hills – one driver we travelled with had to turn off all the passenger lights before using the electric ticket machine because there was not enough power to do both. Another could get his home-made bus bell to ring, but not to stop ringing unless he stopped in the middle of the road, climbed out of his cab and did something with a screwdriver.

But the Maltese passengers are very understanding of these quirks; the islanders tend to have big families and they often work together to customise a bus and provide a job for at least one son (I didn't see any women drivers); it is, as several of them told me, part of their culture.

But try telling that to the EU who notice only that the buses break most known laws relating to health and safely, emissions and disabled access, so that in a few months they will all be gone.

The owner/drivers will be given generous pay-offs and the system will be taken over by a professional bus company which understands the dynamics of meeting customer demand within the constraints of a modern transportation infrastructure.

The Maltese are about to be introduced to Arriva and may God have mercy on their souls.

Shouting-on-Sea

As an occasional travel correspondent, I start from the position that you can't hope to understand foreigners at anything much above Year 9 level and that if you think you do, it's because you don't.

For proof, my partner Lynne and I spent a night in Makarska, a charming Croatian harbour town which we at first mistook for Frinton-on-Sea.

Then, when we were ready for bed, we realised, just our luck, that the all-Croatian shouting championships were being held right outside our window and they obviously went to tie breaks because things didn't quieten down until about 3.30am.

At 6.30am, we were woken by the sound of a large marching band and staggered to the window to see ranks of smartly-uniformed teenage schoolchildren playing percussion and brass instruments with great aplomb. Naturally we thought this was an implausible dream – I mean, the words teenager, smart, aplomb and, in particular, 6.30am… they just don't fit.

But it was all true and occasioned by the fact that it was May Day, so when we walked along the front later in the morning, we had to dodge around mini-rallies organised by various political groups. My favourite was the Croatian Social Democrat Party which offered everyone a free pen and a sardine, which buys my vote any time and I wonder whether Gordon Brown has thought about it.

Lower down the coast, in the stunning city of Dubrovnik, there was a mayoral election going on and walls were plastered with pictures of the candidates – in every case middle-aged men with sculptured grey hair, shiny suits and shifty eyes who you wouldn't trust an inch.

The owner of our hostel, who had been a senior local journalist before deciding it would be more fun to scratch a living with his fishing boat, was a charming and affable man but he turned very serious when I asked him who he might vote for: "You have to understand," he said, "every single one of them is a crook."

Also in Croatia, where we travelled along most of the stunning Dalmatian coast by public bus, we visited the most grim zoo I've ever seen. To get there we had to climb (well, sort of stroll vertically) a great distance up a path leading to the top of a desolate mountain in Split.

I was keen to see the zoo because my holiday reading was Life of Pi by Yann Martel, a novel which contains a spirited defence of zoos and the art of the zookeeper.

But Split zoo is indefensible. A wolf pacing up and down manically, as if in the corridor of a mental-health wing; a big wild boar trying to wallow in the dry, dusty pebbles which make up zoo grounds; an all-alone monkey literally rattling his own cage... even the ordinary, domestic geese

129

and ducks were completely caged in, as if they wanted to escape, which, as Martel explains, no properly-kept zoo animal does, it being a jungle out there.

Life of Pi also reveals that the only truly safe zoo animal – the one that wouldn't even think of giving you the tiniest of nips – is the guinea pig.

The guinea pig enclosure at Split zoo is carpeted with guinea pigs of many generations capering around and breeding like, well, rabbits, as if they think their zoo a wonderful place. I suspect they are deeply stupid.

Afterthoughts

Compiling this book has been an odd experience;
like talking to a person to whom I am closely re-
lated but don't really know.
This is because I seldom re-read my old columns.
I send them out for publication convinced they
are extraordinarily brilliant but when they appear
in print, I generally can't bear to look at them in
case I've deluded myself.
So digging through my files (which mostly con-
sist of gaps) has been interesting – like finding an
old diary you can't remember having written.
Actually, the articles in this book (which isn't a
'best of' collection but more of a 'the ones I
could find' collection) are better than I thought
they would be, although only for negative reasons.
When the Yorkshire Evening Post, back in the
Thatcher years, detailed me to write a weekly column, I set myself the task of making it different
in tone and content from any other column I
knew of. Otherwise what would be the point?
I set out to avoid pontification, pomposity, cheap
populism, pointless alliteration and, most of all,
clichéd words and ideas, which journalism is
prone to, being the only profession, apart from

131

higher management and politics, where clichés
are part of the training.
Every week I set myself the task of avoiding the
obvious, which is harder than you'd think.
Whether I've succeeded is your call (oops, I think
that's a cliché.).
I would just be happy to have earned the epitaph
'at least he tried.'

THE END